Advance Praise

"The portal between life and death is the place between spirit and matter that opens the door to many forms of magic, chief among them, blessings. Martha Halda's *The Fragrance of Angels* does just that, giving us a guided tour of what is bigger than us all."

—Matthew J. Pallamary, author, *Land Without Evil* and *Spirit Matters*

"Martha Halda is a warrior woman! She came back to life fighting for one reason. She needed to mother her two sons . . . on her terms. She did it all in the name of God and for the sake of a mother's love. If you're looking for a heartwarming story chock-full of inspiration, you've found your book."

—Holly Kammier, author, *Kingston Court*, owner, Acorn Publishing

"Seven out of 10 Americans believe in heaven while 58% of us believe in hell, according to the Pew Research Center. The thing is, so few of us have been to either place. In Halda's memoir, she gives us a guided tour of heaven.

"After a horrible car accident in 1999, Halda "passed over" four times. If the parts in San Diego County are interesting, the passages that take place in heaven are fascinating. No matter your religious bent, if you can park your dogmas at the door and let your imagination free, her description of heaven will enthrall. There is even a glimpse of hell if you're paying attention.

"Halda also spent seven weeks in a coma and that recounting is intriguing as well. Halda just tells her story and what she learned without being preachy. So we get to learn along with her the importance of smell, why we should obey the Golden Rule, and that love trumps all."

—*Carlsbad Magazine*

"This true story is a must read for anyone who wants to be inspired by this thing called life, that can be so taken for granted. Martha's account and reflection on this incredible journey will touch you and bring you to tears as you are reminded of the human spirit and teaches us all what is truly important. That is Faith, Family, Hope and Love!"

— Coach John Kentera, radio broadcaster

"Martha was (and still is) the quintessential California girl, long-legged, tan, with a blonde mane and mega-watt smile. Martha was physically my polar opposite and I saw her as a goddess. (I still do.)

"Martha played basketball and ran track in high school and continued running through college. It wasn't until my senior year in college that I discovered my athletic abilities and that's when Martha and I could finally see eye to eye, as athletes!

"Martha shares the exquisite details of her death experience and how she was gifted with a taste of eternity. Through surgeries, a medically induced coma, a long struggle to rehabilitate, the loss of both her parents, and a divorce, Martha relied on her faith and her inner athlete to endure every obstacle.

"We all deserve to create those gold star moments in our lives and to learn to celebrate our abilities. Martha offers the reader a heart-wrenching and spiritually uplifting road map of how she was able to navigate back to life then fight with the courage of an athlete to live life fully with the gifts she received from death.

"Reading *The Fragrance of Angels* reminds me to continually dance in my own light, and once again, I'm awed by my friend and inspirational role model, Martha Halda, the enduring Cali-girl goddess."

—Julie Moss, Ironman triathlete legend and motivational speaker

The Fragrance of Angels

An Accident, a Taste of Eternity, and a New Life

To: Pat

You love us always

been like a

Mother's love.

Love is our

most precious gift we

have to offer.

Love, Martha 2016

a memoir by

Martha Brookhart Halda

Open Books
PRESS

Published by Open Books Press, USA

Open Books
PRESS

www.OpenBooksPress.com
info@OpenBooksPress.com

An imprint of Pen & Publish, Inc.
www.PenandPublish.com
Bloomington, Indiana
(314) 827-6567

Print ISBN: 978-1-941799-40-6
eBook ISBN: 978-1-941799-41-3

Library of Congress Control Number: 2016949601

Printed on acid-free paper.

Acknowledgments

First and foremost to my boys—my life's very special men; Aaron Halda, Nathan Halda, and Miles Oliver . . . you are all good men and I could not be prouder of each of you. I am so glad God gave me you to come back to love. I will always be grateful that I was allowed to return to love and nurture your hearts and souls, and in return, boy, did you nurture mine with the patience you had with me. I will forever love you more than life itself; only for you would I give up Heaven and come back. Yes, but only once.

I greatly appreciate the love, caring, and friendship of so many women who gave me the "girl-power" I needed often during my recovery. First, to my sister Katie Brookhart Peterson, you lady gave me unconditional love. Thank you again and again. Terri Brookhart, for sitting poolside in the hospital all those days, love to you. Next, Cindi Weaver, Chris Wilkerson, Colleen Heublien, Kris Reilly, Margaret Reden, and all my Bunco Ladies sisterhood . . . you were all my super team of support and I am more grateful for your friendship than you will ever know. Sherry Ness, Kelly Crews, and all the Bible study girls, thanks for sharing God's grace.

Thank you to my fellow Ananda College writing class students. We shared so many experiences, perspectives, and heartfelt thoughts of our lives and our spiritual walk. I wish you all the best in life. *Aum, Shanti, Shanti.*

And finally, of course, to Robert Yehling, my friend and love of over fifty years, my "kindergarten nap-pad buddy," I'm deeply grateful. Thank you for the greatest gift of helping me see my highest self, my writing abilities, and the drive to look deeper into recapping my experiences. Your encouragement, advice, and guidance allowed me to not only dream of this book, but the desire to actually write it. Without your personal attention to this project, our fun spiritual adventures, and deep understanding when I would melt down while recalling portions of this story, I would not have been able to do this. I will be forever grateful, and will always love you dearly throughout this life and into the next. You helped me to focus not on what I want or what I've lost, but on what I have; and that is the Peace in knowing the Kingdom of Heaven is within each of us.

Dedication

This book is dedicated to *God*, the author of all things. You gave me not a near-death experience, but rather a taste of eternity.

To my father, *Ray F. Brookhart II*, AKA Pops, you shared with me your faith without ever judging, and you showed inner strength while always being a loving gentleman. You taught me kindness; I look forward to the day when I join you in Heaven.

Most of all, affectionately and lovingly I dedicate this book to my sons, *Aaron G. Halda* and *Nathan C. Halda*. I thank you for your constant support and encouragement during some very difficult times. No boys should have to go through what you did; you both lived up to the character I prayed and wished for you to have when I gave you your names. May you always know how dearly loved you both are by me, Mom. Just as I used to say at your bedtime in the evenings, *I'll love you forever, I'll like you for always, forever and ever my babies you'll be.*

Contents

Prologue

The fresh Himalayan snowmelt near Rishikesh, India, was cold in March, but its sparkling freshness still invited me to frolic, especially since the Ganges River was so clean. That wasn't the case further downstream. I'd just visited the burning Ghats in Varanasi, where they cremated the dead and cast their bodies into this river. The polluted waters there certainly were not inviting. Now, closer to the Himalayans, we were near the headwaters.

It was my fifty-third birthday, and I'd decided to white water raft down the Ganges. A rafting trip worked for me, but not my twenty-something companions. I could not coax any of them into joining me, even when I offered to pay. "It's a chance of a lifetime," I told them. "What better way to celebrate life than to squeeze out every bit of adventure possible?"

They didn't bite on my offer. *Fine.* I was ready and willing to raft along the beautiful banks by myself . . . if only I could get onto the river. My first booked tour canceled, for gender reasons. I was a six-foot Caucasian blonde female, so I didn't exactly blend in well. The tour company official wasn't quite sure what to do with me, since this situation did not happen often. Indian women rarely raft, and certainly never by themselves or with strange men they don't know. Luckily for me, just in the nick of time, two six-foot-tall, adventurous twenty-year-old sisters from Scotland decided to enjoy the views of Rishikesh from the Ganges.

Thank goodness! Now the touring company had three crazy ladies to send down river. We took a thirty-minute drive through the countryside with our guide, whose constant Cheshire grin still is one of the most radiant smiles I've ever seen. We entered the boat and were soon gliding around a bend, where the rapids picked up. From my past experience on the Green River in Utah, I'd say we hit a few category 3 (moderate) and category 4 (difficult) rapids.

After a few minutes, floating and paddling quickly, we en-countered a boat with six large Indian men. A competition ensued. They had the size, age, and body mass—not to mention strength—but we won! This thrilled our smiling guide. In that moment, he knew this ensuing chase with the crazy white ladies would earn the him limelight and attention among his buddies for months. We were money in his popularity account.

We headed swiftly around a turn. "So you ladies want to jump off the cliffs, too?" he asked jokingly.

I had no idea of the height, but it was my birthday, and I like doing memorable things on my birthday. "Yes," I said.

He looked at me like I was crazy. "I was just joking."

"Well, I'm not."

"But I didn't tell you how high it is."

"I don't care; I can do it."

We rounded the bend. The bluff was about thirty to forty feet high. A cluster of men gathered at the edge, measuring with their eyes, trying to figure out how far they would drop, if they jumped. The comical scene reminded me of the Bollywood movie I saw on Christmas Day just two months prior in San Francisco's Haight-Ashbury District. What's more, the guys were taking pictures of each other. It seemed everyone in India constantly took pictures on their phones, documenting each moment of life's adventure.

Time to get ready. My guide made me wear my tennis shoes, a helmet, and a life vest. I didn't want to comply, but when he told me I would not jump otherwise, I gladly strapped up and got out of the raft. I climbed up the bluff, reached the men, watched and listened to their "who will jump first?" show for a few minutes, and then climbed, past them, farther to the next ledge. I walked to the edge—and jumped. The guys stopped their jostling. About twenty pairs of eyes stared in total disbelief as I splashed into the water.

What a thrill! I need more of this. I quickly ascended the cliff, walk past the men to the highest spot, and jumped again. For my third jump, I talked one of the sisters into joining me. By the time we reached the group of men, only one had jumped. Within seconds, we doubled their number, flinging our tall bodies off the edge. When we emerged, one of the men yelled down, "Are you a professional cliff diver?"

They had no idea how happy this made me. "All I did was jump!" I yelled. "Besides, I'm probably the same age as your mother."

I almost didn't make it to be fifty-three. Or forty-one, for that matter. Thirteen years before my cliff jumping moment on the Ganges, I was pronounced clinically dead three times after a terrible car accident in which my SUV landed on top of me. When I survived the emergency surgery and the seven-week induced coma that followed, doctors told my husband, two boys, and family I would probably be a mental vegetable and never walk again. Since that time, I learned how to walk and speak again, endured years of slow recovery, walked a marathon, went through an agonizing divorce, learned new trades, lost jobs and my house, became a college student again, fell in love, and became a writer. I have also begun speaking to groups of all sizes and belief systems for the past several years on my NDE. You know the saying, "Treat every moment or experience like it's your last"? When you face the brink of death—or, in my case, cross over to that side—you really do approach every moment or experience as potentially your last hurrah on earth. At least I did.

I was so proud of my feat. I knew I would see my sweetheart in two days, and I also knew what he would do—tell everyone about my jumps. (Three years later, he still tells them.) He has a knack for identifying the qualities and actions of others, finding the deeper story within, and shares those stories with hearts and souls everywhere. I knew he'd shake his head over my jumps, like he used to do when I bombed down the steep hillsides as a teenager on my skateboard. He would do the same now shaking his head and signal an emphatic, "No!" just as he did whenever I tried to coax him onto the spine-tingling, teeth-rattling roller coasters that I love. Now I was so grateful to be alive, and to celebrate with this thrilling challenge . . . definitely not normal fare for a fifty-third birthday.

As it turned out, Bob waited about an hour after I landed in San Francisco to spread the word. That's how long it was before we saw other people, perfect strangers at that. He whisked me to a nice eatery for my first American meal in a month. When I groggily told him about my cliff jump, he looked over to the people next to us, a couple in their mid-thirties vacationing from St. Louis. One look at them, and it was easy to tell that they adventured through their (probably) young children. "Can you believe she just jumped off thirty-foot cliffs into the Ganges?"

They looked at him, and then me, amazed. "You did?"

I nodded. Bob then cashed in our chips: "She celebrates birthdays in funny ways. This was how she celebrated number fifty-three—jumping off cliffs." (Normally, a girl isn't so eager to have her age revealed to strangers, but he portrayed it as an amazing achievement.)

The Midwestern couple looked over at me, astonished. I wish I could have taken a photo of their shocked faces. Where were all those Indian men with their phone cameras when I needed them?

Finally, the husband said, "I couldn't even imagine cliff jumping any time . . . but you're almost as old as my mother and you did it."

I smiled through burning eyes, the by-product of my twenty-four-hour flight. My inner mind was chanting, *I can, I shall, I will! I can dance in my own spotlight, I shall create my individual life, and I will bask in the light of my abilities within.* However, instead smiling, I laughed and said, "Every moment counts, and it just felt like the right thing to do."

And . . . so does writing this book.

The Accident

October 8, 1999

Blood pours profusely from my ears, smearing across my face. Warm liquid gushes into my chest, my stomach, filling my body with its heaviness; a tingling sensation runs up my legs. I lie on the road, my left leg completely under my body with my foot peeking out above my head. Moments before, I flipped through the air like a rag doll, then my body smashed onto the solid packed dirt road. My head cracked backwards, hitting so hard a sharp searing pain races across the back of my skull.

It's getting so hard to breathe; I can't catch my breath!

In a nearby orange grove, field workers tend the trees and watch. "The lady's SUV careened through the air and flipped several times. We saw her body fly out and the vehicle smash on top of her, and then the car rolled down the bank into the orange trees and the body laid in the road," they later tell the paramedics and police.

From there I had what most people call a near-death experience. I prefer to call it "a taste of eternity."

It happened on Pauma Heights Road, known to locals as Middle Grade or Third Gate. The road ascended with the subtlety of an elevator from my northern San Diego County home and its majestic living room view of Palomar Mountain and its famous observatory. Pauma Heights Road slithered high above expansive avocado and orange groves and ranchos. Along and among the rock-pocked hillsides, turns are tight and the road too steep for a large truck to climb. The road was paved except for a hundred-yard section in front of private property. Boulders three to four feet high flanked that unpaved piece. This was not a hill to run, walk or cycle. (Although in my younger years, I would have tried to bomb it on my skateboard. Wink!)

Or drive, unless you were a thrill seeker or it became neces-sary. Or in my case, someone trying to quickly become a local.

The early evening sun glared harshly on the road. Against this light, sunglasses can only do so much. In the Southern California foothills, October carries with it the brightest and sharpest light of the year, especially when the dry air, cloudless skies and deep-ening shadows meet just before dusk. When I'm in the mood, I sometimes perceive the October sun giving us summer's final warm squeezes before yielding to winter.

I wasn't in the mood. Pauma Heights Road was new to me, along with my big box on wheels, a Ford Expedition SUV, much bigger than the "mommy vans" or midsize luxury cars I was used to driving. Even though my vehicle was touted as a top-of-the-line Eddie Bauer edition, my opinion was "whoop de doo, this thing drives like a truck." I had complained about it, several times, to the guys at Bates Nut Farm, where I helped out. "This thing is so squirrelly, I don't like it at all," I'd said.

On top of that, I had only driven Pauma Heights Road a few times since my oldest son, Aaron, started high school a month earlier. With that concern at the back of my mind, I ascended the hill, only to be blinded by the harsh light and glare of the October sun. Afraid I might plow head-on into another car, I veered to the right, toward the line of boulders. I knew a couple of high school boys drove this road on their way home from football practice, and I certainly didn't want to run into them.

The glare quickly filled my windshield. I wanted to get out of the center of the road, where the boys might be. I wanted to be able to see them. I was not familiar with this road or my new car.

I had to make a choice, and fast: Do I expose myself to a possible head-on collision with a car I couldn't see? Or do I drive toward the right of the shoulder, and risk crashing or bumping my new car into one of those boulders?

I veered right—

—and hit the boulders. The car spun and flipped end-over-end, with me inside. It spun so wildly front to back that it created a centrifugal force, which pulled on my body with incredible power. I couldn't see through the glaring sun, and gripped the steering wheel so tightly it felt as if my fingers would explode, hoping I would not be thrashed so badly. It felt hopeless. I yelled out, "God, oh God, please help me!" very loudly, a plea from deep in the center of my soul. A prayer of this depth had never been uttered by me before.

I lost my grip. Despite wearing my seat belt, the force of the ensuing impact threw me from the car. Did I crash through the driver's side window? Did the door fly open? Did I sail through the windshield? I still don't know, and I'm not sure anyone else truly does, either. I always buckled up, from the moment I had become a mother, but somehow I broke free. Doctors later told me I suffered tissue damage around my hips consistent with having worn a seat belt.

Suddenly, I was lying on the road.

This is where divine providence stepped in. I used to believe that situations, circumstances, and sudden events in life were either accidents or coincidences, but I was about to learn something new. The *Webster's Dictionary* defines "providential" as, "Things that happen because of God's sustaining power and guiding human destiny." The dictionary describes "coincidence" as, "Events that happen at the same time by accident." I now believe there is no such thing as an accident. Everything arises from providence. If we choose to see life this way, we will have an easier road in it. Now I want to feel God's cautionary taps on my shoulder and not wait for the sledgehammer to squash me from a supposed accident, deception . . . or heartbreak.

How did I end up on Middle Grade? At about 4:30 p.m., Aaron called to be picked up after football practice. I left my younger son, eleven-year-old Nathan, at home because he complained of a sudden stomachache. To leave Nathan home alone flowed against my conscience, but he appeared to be pretty sick. Also, as he confidently informed me, he was "an eleven-year-old, a sixth grader in junior high, and you need to learn to cut the cord, Mom." Hmmm. His words were enough, but for emphasis, he rolled his eyes and huffed as he stomped loudly down the hallway to his room. So I decided to cut the cord. For a day.

My plan was to pick up Aaron, drive the twenty minutes home for dinner, and then drive back to the Valley Center High School football stadium for that evening's game, where I volunteered to work the snack bar at that evening's game. So I drove off, leaving Nathan at home.

I can't help but think what likely would have happened if Nathan had ridden with me. I have run this scenario through my brain again and again, thinking just how blessed we were and fortunate that he was sick and needed to stay home. If he had been in the car with me, he might not be here now. I would never again receive his love and support that I'm lucky enough, thank God, to still be able to enjoy.

Then God stepped in. This was the first sign of providence I took note of.

A man in his wife's car drove over the hill. He approached the accident and called 911—a rarity in 1999 when cell phones were not yet must-have items. Not only that, but cell phone reception was very weak, if not impossible in this rural area (I had never gotten reception there . . . ever). Philip Stone quickly drove to a higher point on the road, stopped the car and tried to remember where his wife Marianne had stashed the new car phone. (She shared this story with me 14 years later, after I shared my taste of eternity with the fourth, fifth, and sixth grade catechism class of my friend Kathy Eckert at Valley Catholic Church). The Stones had just moved out to the country and she wasn't feeling so safe yet—hence the phone. But she was afraid that if a field worker or unsavory person saw it, they might break into the car and steal it. So she stashed it in an uncommon place for a cell phone.

As he reached the high point of the road, Philip slowed to a stop. *Where did she put that thing?* Then, as Philip later told me, he felt an energy or presence guiding his hand. He reached deep under the driver's seat, and realized his hand was firmly planted on the phone. Grabbing it out from beneath the seat, he dialed 911. Soon, an ambulance was on its way. Providence or coincidence?

After calling 911, Philip motioned for a car heading the other way to slow down. He stopped the car, mentioned the wreck to the driver, and cautioned that I was a mess. "It doesn't look like the person is going to make it," he said to the other driver.

I heard those words. My body lay fifty yards away, my hearing suddenly more acute for whatever reason, but there was nothing I could do about it. I couldn't move, and I couldn't breathe.

Just then, providence waved her blessed wing again. The driver of the second car turned out to be Rob Gilster, a family friend and head football coach at Valley Center High. On game days, Rob followed a personal custom of driving home, eating dinner, and opening his Bible to find a passage to use as motivation to lead his team to victory. He chose his reading by closing his eyes, opening to a random page, and reading the verses that awaited him. You know how this usually works: We usually land on something that gives us some benefit, guidance, comfort, or solace.

Not this time. The reading distressed Rob, but he kept lurching forward, trusting and believing this was what God wanted him to read:

So from the brink of death shall I bring you forward.

The reading depressed Rob more than it uplifted him. How would he incorporate it into his pregame motivational talk? He had no idea, but trusted the solution would come to him as he drove Pauma Heights Road to the stadium.

When Rob arrived at the scene, he did not recognize the woman whose face was covered in blood and dirt. He raced back to his truck to find a blanket and cover the poor woman. As he walked away, my body shook, and I started to go into shock. My eyes rolled back in my head, and I couldn't catch my breath. After Rob returned, he became nauseous as he saw the unnatural way my body was contorted. My leg folded completely underneath my body, and my foot jutted out behind my head, as if I had toes growing out of my skull. I do have long legs, long enough for this to happen, but this is one "yoga" posture I won't be trying again! He couldn't believe a body could bend this way, and desperately wanted to return my leg to its full, upright position. However, he feared touching me, knowing it might cause further damage and pain.

He started to pray for me . . . rather, the poor, unidentifiable injured woman. I know that he prayed, because I could *feel* his every plaintive word deeply. His eyes wandered for a moment, and he saw the crushed Ford Expedition. "That looks like Martha's new car," he muttered to himself.

Rob bent down to wipe blood and dirt from my face—and finally recognized me.

I can't imagine what he thought as he watched me gasping for air and life. He kept praying—and I kept feeling it, in every cell of my being, a being that was opening quickly into the beauty of eternity.

Chapter 2

The Mercy Air Angel

Even as I gasped for air, I lay in total peace.

When the EMTs arrived, the only other person with me was Rob. He remained with me on the road when the paramedics arrived, praying and urging me to live. I felt all of his emotions, as surely as I feel my own every day. The paramedics assessed my situation and called for a second ambulance. The EMTs in the second ambulance quickly realized, just as the first responders had, that there was no way they would keep me alive long enough to reach the hospital by ambulance. They called in the Mercy Air Life Flight Helicopter, which arrived within minutes to airlift me to Palomar Pomerado Hospital in Escondido.

I later learned that I was pronounced legally dead four times, but one time, I revived so quickly they removed it from my record. One official pronouncement occurred during my time on the road, again in flight to the hospital, and yet again while on the operating table.

Not that I was sticking around . . .

The term "near death" is an oxymoron to me. It's not a "near-death" experience, but rather a wetting of the appetite, a taste of eternity, an actual encounter of the reality to which our soul and consciousness move after death, the feeling of life's emotions, and an all-encompassing experience of the beauty and love that fills Heaven. A place where all possibilities, colors, and perceptions fill every inch of our being, it's the paradise we hear about in churches, from the lips of pastors, and read about in the words of the Bible and so many other sacred books. The place where we believe our souls go for their final rest, but where so much more actually begins. *Heaven.*

I know this firsthand.

When I passed over the first time, I felt an incredible rush of anguish from Rob. "The life flight paramedics had worked prepping you on the road, so they were able to transfer you to the gurney and into the helicopter," he later told me. "The engines were started and I was anxious and ready to watch them take off, finally, sending you on your way, but suddenly, the blades were turned off. I watched the cops and paramedics start packing up, and I saw a stillness fill their faces.

"I found one of the guys and asked, 'Why have they turned off the blades?'

"The paramedic hesitated, not wanting to upset me. 'The blades are turned off when the person inside is gone. They can't transport; they have to wait for the coroner.'"

While I was engulfed in Rob's anguish, I started to feel things on a different sensory level. As my physical body lay on the road, and then in the helicopter, I still smelled the dirt of the road—and watched the sky.

At that moment, I realized something: *My body was there . . . down there, on terra firma . . . but I wasn't.*

I lay there looking into this fabulous sky. Suddenly, a star shot toward me incredibly fast. It seemed to travel from somewhere in the cosmos, light years away. Then it grew closer. As it neared to within three hundred feet, I realized it wasn't a star at all, but an Angel . . . my Guardian Angel. My only previous connection with angels came from the cherub and fairy type found in card stores. I had never read any stories of angels and wasn't really sure I believed in them. Certainly, I had read parts of the Bible that described them, but these descriptions seemed like something for times long ago, not present-day.

My view today is entirely different.

The sky took on the complexion of twilight, even though it was just after 4:30 p.m. A soft periwinkle blue swirled with splashes of turquoise and the lightest of white clouds. Spinning stars dotted the sky, causing the heavens to spin, and the stars lined out with vibrational tails around each of them. It reminded me of Vincent Van Gogh's painting *The Starry Night*, which had always been one of my favorites. (A dozen years later, while attending college, I painted a pastel depiction of *The Starry Night* for my inspirational art class. I ended up selling the painting to the college—my first sale. It wasn't a big sale, but that wasn't the meaning. I was trying to duplicate the vibration of energy emanating from the sun/Son and the stars when I passed over.)

The Angel, my Angel, raced from this translucent sky. As she neared my body, she slowed to a rocking flow, assuring me of her love. How she comforted me! She let me know I shouldn't be afraid, that she was there for me and loved me.

She wore a long, A-line cut gown made out of shimmering silver fabric similar to raw silk. The gown reached to her ankles, had long bell-shaped sleeves, and a high neck fitted bodice The chest panel was filled with the most intricate and awesome embroidery my eyes had ever seen. The thread appeared to be made of real silver. Her gown shown so brilliantly it was white like a flash of lightning.

My Angel had no halo above her head, but rather, an intensely warm golden glow surrounding, embracing, and emanating from all around her. As I looked at this beautiful Angel, her face and form, I focused on every detail. She was so hypnotic and so beautiful. I felt that the light that emanated from her was too bright to be viewed with human, or rather earthly, eyes. Her hair was shoulder length, a wavy light brown with blonde flecks. Her face was like that of a child right before puberty, with androgynous features. She was neither male nor female. You know how the face of a youth can show either a boy's or girl's expressions, depending on how you look at them? This was exactly the same.

She had wings . . . WOW, what wings! They started at the back of her shoulders, arched up to the base of her head, and then tapered down to below her knees. They were iridescent; I could see through them. Their coloring a stunning opalescent. They seemed to consist of a feather-like substance, yet weren't like a bird at all. They carried such beauty and a feeling of complete normalcy, like they should be part of everyone's body.

The most wonderful music accompanied her, a mixture of chimes, a cello, song, praises, and a rushing sound. I later recognized the rushing as the sound of the life flight helicopter's blades. This music was soothing to all my needs. I would imagine each soul hears a certain music or melodic beat that fills them. I can't imagine the music that sooths me would be the same for, say, my parents, and certainly not that of my children, yet it seemed to be universal and timeless. The tempo matched that of my heartbeat, messaging, and pounding as it trumpeted through me. Just like seeing the Angel's holy glow or halo was too bright for human eyes, this music was far too loud to be heard with human ears.

In addition, the most incredible floral scent surrounded her. Or, to be more precise, it saturated her. It smelled like the most fragrant garden on a hot summer day, or the best perfume scent. As I swallowed every bit of this awesome fragrance, I danced back to my youth. The fragrance reminded me of a summer when I was about six. My grandmother, Grand Mary, was visiting from Idaho; we were in the Balboa Park Rose Garden in San Diego. It was a very hot day. Thousands of roses emitted every scent in the book, it seemed. They released their sweetness to the smoldering summer sun.

This wondrous scent that now immersed and embraced me was more intense. The scent of Heaven, incorporated the freshness of rain, earthiness of a mountain meadow, the calming effect of lavender as it opens the chakra at the point between my eyebrows (the Christ Center), sweetness of an orchard of orange blossoms, and so many other floral smells. This scent was alive! It danced! It sparkled and swirled as it embraced me! I felt lathered and dipped into the intoxication of a tuberose, the softness of plumeria, and the full blush of freesia.

The memories of these scents remained in my cells after I came back from my taste of eternity. For years, I wore "Tea Rose" perfume. Recently, while strolling a shopping mall I was pulled, by a scent so pure, across the store to the Estée Lauder counter, and I was drawn back to my time in Heaven by a full-body Tuberose-Gardenia floral perfume. I was drawn to the counter, searching for the bottle that was offering the source of the scent of Heaven. I smiled at the counter women, *I need to know where it's coming from,* too nervous to tell her the "it" was the smell of Heaven. I zeroed in; yes, this was it: Private Collection Tuberose-Gardenia . . . Heaven. While "Private Collection" is too costly for me now, this perfume sits high on my wish list. A girl does need to have those pretties to motivate her!

A friend told me that somewhere the Bible refers to the "aroma or scent of Christ." It is the only thing I can imagine could ever smell that wonderful!

I was not greeted by anyone other than my Angel. She let me know I shouldn't be afraid, that she was there for me and she loved me. To know I wasn't alone . . . I had never felt more soothed, nurtured in my soul, fearless, or secure. When I describe this today I say, "Take the most incredible love you've ever felt, the most sumptuous scent, the most vibrant rainbow of colors, the perfect temperature, and amplify it by the thousands, and you'll come sort of close, but even that doesn't describe the beauty."

This is the beautiful realization I always carry deeply in my heart and life: we are not left alone! I was being held so lovingly by someone I couldn't see with my eyes, but could only feel and perceive. What unbelievable love and strength! It felt the way a baby must feel when being cradled in its mother's arms for the first time. How awesome is that!

Through all of this, I remained aware of the accident and yet didn't feel any pain.

I traveled into the sky with my Angel. She was not holding me, although she was very close, maybe an arm's length away. Somehow, instinctively, I knew God was cradling me in his arms; a most amazing feeling of love filled every cell of my body. The only thing in this life that I can relate it to was the look in my sons' eyes as they peered into mine that first moment I held them after their births. They wiggled and flashed the sort of knowing smile that says, yes, I was the voice that they had become accustomed while in my womb.

We traveled upward, through a vortex of some sort. It wasn't really a tunnel, but I can see how other people might describe it that way. Nor was it a physical vortex, like the energy vortexes at certain places on Earth; it was more like a vacuum tube. It reminded me of the view from a jet as you speed past clouds, except I was rushing vertically upward into the sky, not flying horizontally through it. To me, a tunnel is solid, but as I shot upward, I could see beyond this tube-like space while being filled with sheer awe of the astounding beauty there was to behold. The law of gravity was suspended. I viewed the most stunning astral planes, skies, and landscapes. The magnificent skies and landscapes were vibrating in every color and shade, and then some. I felt the colors in my body cells . . . only I knew my body wasn't with me, but down in the helicopter. I was traveling in my soul, which absorbed the colors, beauty, and warmth.

This marked the beginning of a new ability to feel someone's feelings directly, as opposed to merely hearing about them.

A Place I Never Expected to Be
. . . The Ledge of Review

My Taste of Eternity intensifies.

My Angel and I travel into the sky. We rise to a couple hundred feet above the ground, and I gaze down to Rob. He stands next to a paramedic team still trying to revive me. Overwhelming grief floods through him; he looks like a broken man who, minutes before, was a strapping six-foot-five hulk.

I feel his pain, more than I feel my own body. For some reason, I now possess the ability to experience the pure feeling of another person, to absorb their emotions as if they were my own feelings. *Wow!* Then I realize I can pass my thoughts onto him, from soul to soul: *Rob, hurry, don't be upset, hurry, we . . . we are going to Heaven!* I try to persuade him to hurry and catch up with me.

As I do, my Angel gently touches my shoulder. We instantly rush higher and higher above the body sprawled out on Pauma Heights Road.

This is so much different than my beliefs about the after-life or near-death experiences. For years, I held an Old Testament vision of God the Almighty, sitting on his throne with bolts of lightning shooting from His crown, while he shamed new arrivals to Heaven with fear, not love. I also expected when I died and passed over to

Heaven, I would meet my Grandmary, other relatives, or friends that had passed away. I envisioned Heaven as quiet and solemn, a grand library or monastery where we prayed and meditated with the stillness of cloistered monks. As for angels? I never acknowledged them as real, even though I loved pictures of them and the beautiful, magical qualities we created for them.

Yet here I am, traveling with my Guardian Angel, drifting, floating, like watching a butterfly or hummingbird. I receive no visit from lost family or loved ones, nor a rush of strangers and old friends welcoming me.

My mind runs through every description of Heaven I ever read in the Bible, different scriptures. In a flash of perception, I remember everything we talked about in Church, how some people said that the only way we enter Heaven is through our death. Our final, good-bye-world-forever death. Everything else, many say, is a figment of the imagination. Or hallucinations, as many neurologists and neurosurgeons believe. (I would hear about this several times later.)

So, if I am not dead, if I cannot experience Heaven, if near-death and after-life experiences are fanciful stories and hallucinations, then why am I with an Angel? Why am I flying toward Heaven? Am I *dead*?

My Angel and I travel further from earth and higher, toward the stars. An electric energy charges my body. I float in a complete state of calmness, and experience the most beautiful landscapes as they pass into view. I not only observe them, but also feel a part of them, how they connect to me. I hear, smell, and see every aspect of these landscapes within every cell of my being. I feel as though I am wearing 3-D glasses in an IMAX theater, absorbing scenes and soundtracks. Only my "glasses" are sensory perceptions, and the "movie" is the indescribable environment surrounding me.

Suddenly, my Angel delivers me to a stunning meadow beyond anything I have ever seen on earth. What a place! It occurs to me that every cell or atom of this heavenly landscape contains its own all-inclusive life, emanating the highest praises toward the Creator of it all.

I'm reminded of a hiking trip I took two summers before, to the base of the Matterhorn in Zermatt, Switzerland. Picture Julie Andrews twirling and singing in an Alpine meadow, all four octaves of her magnificent voice celebrating the day. While hiking with my (then) husband, we reached a meadow with a similar look and feel to that of the opening scene in *The Sound of Music*. (I would visit the actual meadow where that filming took place in 2015.) As we hiked through the Swiss Alps, ringing bells echoed across the countryside from what I thought were centuries-old churches, creating wonderful music. Only they were not church bells, but the bells around the necks of cows roaming the meadows. "The hills are alive with the sound of music," my husband sang, over and over, breaking into a smile as he twirled around, pirouetting like a rather large ballerina, his arms stretched out. Not quite Julie Andrews, in appearance or voice, but it touched me how the beauty of the meadow overwhelmed him. Even the mountain goats lifted their grass-filled mouths and took notice.

This heavenly meadow bursts with a more intense and immediate depth of life. I find I can immerse my soul into any blade of grass, glisten of water, or leaf of tree and not only feel it, but merge with it. I focus and rub my eyes, not sure if what I'm seeing matches what I feel. *Is this real?* I peer into every cell and atom within the meadow. The vibration carried within and broadcast from the trees, grass, flowers, cliffs, and water . . . amazing. The varieties of color in each plant far exceed anything on Earth. I perceive millions of colors, far beyond any rainbow or sunset I have ever seen. Stunning!

The meadow perches atop a steep mountain, ending with a ledge that drops thousands of feet. I feel I'm placed there as a holding area of sorts, while my "case," so to speak, is looked over—reviewed. I stand, or hover, next to the ledge, almost on top of it . . . now slipping from it. I remain calm, not the least bit afraid. *Strange.*

At that instant, through a deeper intuition and feeling, what I can best describe as a form of ESP intimates that it is not my time to remain in Heaven. *What? I don't want to go back!*

I realize the meadow is only a holding area of sorts. I want it to hold me, the way my loving man holds me—warmly, fully, for somewhere in the neighborhood of forever. I want to lie in the lushest grasses I've ever seen and absorb the warm sun on my body (I love lying in the sun!). About this sun? It hits me instantly, like every other perception right now: This is the *Heavenly Son*.

My keen salesmanship skills take over, beginning with Rule Number One: overcome all objections. In other words, *don't take no for an answer*. I barter with my Angel, begging to stay. I reach out to whomever will listen—God, Jesus, my Angel—that my time is *Now*. My pleas pulse through my soul: *I'm not supposed to go back!*

We fly upward again, farther than before, arriving this time into a grander space. Free. *It has worked*, I promise myself. *God has heard my plea!* my soul shouts aloud.

This meadow stretches to the size of a major league baseball field, but shaped like two fields sewn together into a half circle. The tall grasses in the middle of the meadow flow and sing. The valley shifted around to satisfy my wildest fancy of trees and flowers. Gold in Nature, what a great pleasure!

When the occasional flower pops up, my nostrils fill instantly with its scent. I look intently into the center of a creamy white flower with a deep purple center; its magnificent fragrance recalls the tropical floral smells of Kauai. It reminds me of a particular favorite saying: "God smiles through the faces of flowers." I blink—and find myself lying among them, smack in the middle of this lovely garden.

A perfect breeze blows at a perfect temperature, the air cleaner and clearer than the highest mountain air I've ever breathed. I want to sway with the grasses. The little girl, me, dancing freely in the field is not quite awake yet as to why I'm here in this valley.

The meadow rolls out to a grove of trees that offers shade and coolness. A deep purple mountain range vaults above the edge of the trees. The exquisite energy of these natural wonders fills me with warmth and love. *How lovely it would be*, I think, *if this place had a waterfall. Voilà!* Cells from each portion of the meadow, grasses, trees, mountains and flowers swiftly shift together, right before my eyes, and transform into a robust waterfall. How is it that my every intention or hope manifests into instant reality? This happens over and over again.

As I gaze across the meadow, the purple features, especially the mountains, send a sort of shockwave to fill my soul with an encompassing, Divine Love—the very Love of God. The Love calms and fills every emotional need I ever felt. It vibrates through my body, starting from my heart, and travels up and down my spine before spreading into my skin, and then well beyond my form. Some deep forms of meditation approach this state, but the difference is a meditator is still physically connected to his or her body. Furthermore, only God can lift us through the final step to Heaven.

Not only am I surrounded by this Love, but I am wrapped and embraced within its magnificent energy. A new lesson, a new understanding, a new knowledge transmits into me: *I am with God.*

As quickly as the revelation hits me, a video flashes through my mind at the speed of light. Make that the speed of thought. I watch frame after frame of the actions and moments of all forty years of my life, feeling and perceiving the positive and negative aspects of my actions. I'm shown via imagery, a type of ESP, which includes all the human senses. With each scene, or experience, I am reminded of not only how I felt, but also more important—and surprising—how *the other person felt.*

It's one thing to treat someone nicely, carrying out acts of kindness that leaves him or her feeling more loved. Those actions create pleasant moments in this life review. However, everything changes when I see actions of mine that hurt another person—in any way. If I criticized someone heavily, I actually feel much more than the sharpness of my words. I *see* the impact of those words. What if the other person drove home, got into an argument with their kids, and the kids didn't speak to them for weeks? I feel that pain, any action of mine that affected them, their feelings toward me, others, or most importantly toward themselves—*in every way my initial action affected the other person. I really* feel it.

Luckily, I hurt very few people. I believe in love and in resolving conflict, and I try to dissolve any arguments that come my way. I can't begin to explain the feeling of watching myself hurt another soul in this setting. As it is, I feel the pain of my wrong actions throughout my body, even when I am shown moments where I chose between being a great friend, or going my own way—and went my own way. Excruciating.

My review feels tediously slow. *When will it end?* I start to detest myself for causing unease and discomfort to others. Never has the Golden Rule felt more real. Then I realize that all the painful acts I watch, and experience again, are transgressions for which I never asked for forgiveness.

I vow to think out the potential consequences of my actions before taking them. Now when I inadvertently hurt or wrong somebody, I ask for forgiveness directly from the person. (Sometimes I have the guts.) Other times, I pray to receive it. Thankfully, I was raised to understand that no one is better than anyone else, just that they might sit in a better place . . . today. Who knows what tomorrow brings? I yearn to treat people the way I want to be treated, to be aware of their life circumstances and challenges, and then to act accordingly, with compassion and respect. The Golden Rule. I hang onto it for dear life. I try to adhere to it more than ever.

As the review winds down, one desire overwhelms my being: *I do not want to feel this way ever again.*

Why the review? I respect its purpose. It brings me to a deep peace and thorough understanding of my life before I can move on to learn more. It reaches me like a voice I cannot hear, nor see, but I can understand; it is an extra-sensory transmission of experience.

God readies me for what, I'm certain, is next: going to Heaven and never returning to earth. I lay in the grass, absorbing what I have seen and felt, and what I can learn once He takes me the rest of the way Home.

My mind is still shouting, *I am supposed to stay right here in this wonderful meadow, with this wonderful Angel forever.*

I feel a void next to me. I look through the meadow, the trees, the mountains and waterfall . . . and she's gone.

Where did she go?

Instantly, I miss her deeply. Very deeply. *How can I miss someone so deeply so fast?* But, I do. What has happened to my beautiful Angel?

As it turns out, I make a return visit much sooner than anyone expects.

A Providential
Football Game

"What is taking her so long? Sorry dude, this sucks. We've been waiting for her way too long," Aaron grumbled.

He and Andrew, his friend, waited. And waited. And waited . . .

They stood in front of the Valley Center High School gym, near the lower parking lot, their freshman football practice having finished. They high-fived their teammates, milled around, and tried to learn all the Who-What-When-Where for that evening's post-game activities. The upperclassmen wouldn't give them the time of day. Only a few months before, as eighth graders, they relished their perch atop the campus totem pole. They missed being Mr. Big.

The parking lot buzzed with cars heading out and their drivers heading home, to restaurants, to friends' houses . . . wherever they ventured, knowing it was only a few hours until game time. Eventually, the hubbub quieted to a low drone. Only a few cars remained.

Aaron stood with Andrew, whom he'd invited over to the house for video games, some skateboarding, and dinner. They were anxious to get home and have fun before returning to Valley Center High for the game. They watched with some interest as an ambulance sped past, turned right and headed to the crest of Pauma Heights Road, sirens ablaze, the driver flooring it.

Aaron looked at Andrew. "Wonder what's up," he said. "Nothing ever happens out here in the boonies."

He grew more impatient, a common trait with my oldest. He called home and left three messages, each taking on a firmer tone. Finally, he turned to Andrew. "Sorry man, this is getting ridiculous."

Another ambulance roared up Cole Grade Road, past the high school. Just like the earlier one, it turned right onto Pauma Heights Road. Two police cars followed behind, their sirens squealing and lights flashing. *Cops out here?* Then a helicopter raced overhead. "Must be some big drug bust or something," Andrew joked.

A sinking feeling gripped Aaron's stomach. The kid had always carried a strong sixth sense, which I always encouraged him to trust. For me, a strong sixth sense is like having an extra compass to navigate through life. He swallowed hard. "Dude, you better call your mom to come get you." He pointed up at the helicopter. "I think those guys are going to help my mom."

The helicopter hovered, then circled over the location where the ambulances stopped. Aaron and Andrew watched from a distance as the helicopter's downdraft kicked up a hurricane funnel of dust, plainly visible from the high school parking lot. Though Aaron knew the helicopter had touched down at the section of the road I never liked to drive, he also knew I was rarely late. I always arrived within a few minutes of the agreed-upon time. Like every caring mom trying to be in three places at once, I scrambled. After fourteen years of daily practice, I walked the time tightrope like a Cirque du Soleil acrobat.

A few minutes later, after he'd prayed over my inert body on the scene, Rob Gilster rushed by the school parking lot. He noticed Aaron and dropped his eyes, not making eye contact. He was crying. Hard! Aaron later shared with me, "He didn't even crack one of his usual half-corny, half-funny jokes."

"Hey Gilster, what's up?" Aaron asked.

No response.

Aaron's gut tightened. *Something's really wrong.*

Rob had known Aaron since he was three. We used to be neighbors, our two-acre properties touching at one corner. Aaron spent countless hours playing with the Gilster kids. Rob's wife, Robin, and I volunteered for all sorts of activities. We were suckered into doing things for community groups—always.

We took our little guys to Moms Together, a weekly women's Bible study for mothers of preschoolers. As our boys grew, we carried our volunteerism into working the snack bars of Little League, junior high and high school basketball, and of course high school football. I joked that I had a *V* or *S* engraved in my forehead, depending on the day and activity: *V* for volunteer, and *S* for sucker.

As he watched Rob try hard to control his emotions, Aaron's suspicions grew that I'd been in an accident. He was fighting with the feeling in his gut, trying not to believe it, when a school security guard drove up in a golf cart. "Please come with me," he said.

"What's up, dude?"

"I don't know. I was just told to bring you to the office."

Aaron turned to Andrew and croaked out, "Call your mom, dude,"as he huffed and followed the guard.

When he arrived at the principal's office, Aaron knew what they were going to say, but he still needed to hear it. "So was that my mom they flew out there for?" he asked.

The principal wouldn't answer.

Moments later, Aaron's grandmother arrived. Still nothing. Aaron kept asking. No one would answer. "This is bullshit!" he yelled, now irate. It takes a lot to piss off Aaron, but once he's there . . . "I know it's my mom, so why won't you guys tell me anything?"

The principal explained that they needed to wait for the sheriff deputies to arrive. School policy prohibited him from saying anything, he added.

That comment revved up my son. He kept asking, his voice growing louder, slinging profanities around the room. Then he punched a wall, shocking everyone. This was not consistent with Aaron's personality, at least not away from the basketball court. On the court, he was extremely competitive. Right down to dishing on his own mother. During one game, a kid drained a twenty-foot jump shot. I jumped up and cheered. I appreciate good plays, especially in basketball, my favorite sport. Unfortunately for me, the boy played for the other team. Aaron stopped running midcourt, looked up into the stands, pure irritation hardening his face: *Really, Mom?* He didn't have to say it. I could feel it.

Finally, a sheriff's deputy arrived. "Your mother is in a critical situation," he said. "She is being life-flighted to Palomar Pomerado Hospital."

Meanwhile, my eleven-year-old, Nate, sat at home alone, nursing a stomachache. He was supposed to accompany me to pick up Aaron from school, but he stayed in bed, hoping for my return. In our family we take care of each other, and that is something he always looked forward to when he was sick. You can only imagine how I feel about this decision now. His stomachache saved his life.

From his room, Nate heard Aaron leave three frantic phone messages. He snuggled deeper under his covers. He could hear the distant squeal of sirens and different pitches of the ambulance, fire trucks, and the police cars. Nate wondered what was going on. When the phone rang a fourth time, he decided to answer. He ran down the long tiled hallway to the living room, and caught the last ring before voice mail.

It was a nurse at Palomar Pomerado Hospital. They asked Nate if his father was home.

"No," Nate said. "He's out."

"How old are you?" the nurse asked.

"Eleven."

"Is there an adult there with you?"

"No, but my mom will be home soon."

There was a brief pause. "This is Palomar Pomerado Hospital," the nurse said, her tone calm but urgent. "We have critical information concerning your mother, and we need to contact your father and any other family members that are available."

I kept my address book next to the phone. Nate opened it and flipped to the *Bs*—the Brookharts. My family. He ran a shaking finger down the list: Grammy and Grampy, Aunt Katie, Uncle

Chris, Uncle Tim, and Uncle David. After he gave the nurse that information, he flipped to the *H*s and provided his Dad's cell number, plus home numbers for his Grandmother and Uncle Jimbo.

The nurse asked which family member lived the closest to Escondido. "My Grandmother lives right down the street from us. The rest of the family is in Carlsbad."

"Thank you."

I later considered that nurse an angel. She treated Nate as though he was in his twenties, not a scared-to-death eleven-year-old boy. Because of that, Nate responded like an adult. He reached deep into his being and conjured up the strength to keep it together and give the nurse all the information she needed.

About forty-five minutes later, Grandma and Aaron arrived at the house. They picked up Nate and sped to the hospital.

Providence again played a big part in the first hour, the golden hour, after the helicopter delivered me to Palomar Pomerado.

The previous week, at the homecoming football game, I hawked game programs in the opponents' bleachers. We were playing the team from the neighboring town, where much of my tennis life took place. My competitive nature took over. (So *that's* where Aaron got it!) I figured, *Why not see how many of these homecoming programs I can sell to the enemy?* I baited the San Pasqual High fans by telling them, "Our homecoming court rocks . . . and yours?" and "Don't you want to see how our queen and princesses rate, compared to yours?"

I sold more programs than anyone else. While proving my prowess, I also saw several of my tennis-playing friends, one of whom introduced me to her husband, Dr. David Cloyd.

Guess which emergency room surgeon happened to be on call at Palomar Pomerado when I arrived?

In the past, I would have considered Dr. Cloyd's presence a coincidence. Not anymore. There is no such thing. My Angel had just shown me how all things are connected. I had just seen and felt it first-hand. Despite a long day, Dr. Cloyd took one look at me and immediately scrubbed up. He would make the long shot attempt to put this six-foot blonde Humpty Dumpty back together again.

At about the same time, Rob Gilster took the microphone at halftime and asked the large Valley Center High football crowd for a moment of silence to pray for me. What a day for Rob: finding my crushed body on the scene, not recognizing me at first, running into a then-unaware Aaron at school, and somehow having to block out watching the paramedics pronounce me dead and then prepare his team for the big game.

Among the game fans was the new pastor of Valley Center Community Church, John Sale. The previous Sunday, I introduced myself to Pastor Sale by my first and last name. Summer and early autumn services were held outside, he was new to the church, and I didn't stick around often after services, so we hadn't met until this introduction. After Pastor Sale heard Rob's announcement of my accident and observed the moment of silence, knowing I was one of his flock, he rushed to the hospital. Why did I introduce myself to the pastor using my full name, just the week before, when normally I use just my first name? Coincidence? Or Providence?

When Pastor Sale arrived at Palomar Pomerado, he wasn't alone. The waiting room filled with nearly a hundred people during the evening, all praying for my survival and trying to get word on my condition.

They didn't know it at the time, and neither did I, but my condition as they were asking was this: The doctors and I were fighting for my life. My body lay on the operating table, and I had just left it. Again.

To the Bright Light of God

Doctor Cloyd does not hear any of the noises that fill the Acute Trauma operating room. Like a focused athlete in the zone, everything leaves his awareness except my heart, which he zeroes in on. It's not beating. Hope, urgency, and intensity fill his body in equal measures; I can feel it. I'm trying to help him let me go, release me, send me on my way. I want to see more of Heaven.

Instead, I feel his intention and desire to save me. The doctor reaches inside my rib cage, and stretches his hands into the left side of my chest. He's gripping downward, his fingers pumping, manipulating my heart in his hands and trying to get me started again. Around him stand attending nurses and other assistants, along with an array of medical instruments. I watch all of this from above my body, above the room. I'm looking down at my body, not physically nor emotionally attached. It was a nice body, it served me well, and I'm now ready for the next step. I don't need it any longer.

I passed over one more time.

Doctor Cloyd moved ahead with the eight-hour surgery, which began when he used a type of rib cracker, a sort of Jaws of Life, to crank open my torso so the surgery team would be able to work. I'm not a doctor and don't know the medical terminology for this late twentieth-century wonder, but . . . I will be forever glad the contraption existed. He split me from right below my breastbone to just above my pelvis, cracking me open like a pumpkin to get a peek at the mess inside. I can only imagine how stunned he was by what he found: ribs smashed literally into pieces, raw edges that completely ripped up my lungs, which had their own problems: They'd burst open from pressure. The surgical team had to stitch my lungs back together piece by piece, reducing them to about one quarter of their normal size; fortunately for me, lungs regenerate themselves. My hips and pelvis were fractured in six different places, due to the force of the Ford Expedition smashing me. When my left leg bent backward underneath my body, it permanently strained my nerves. The nerves and blood vessels are separate, until the point where the hip joins the leg, where they blend as one. Now damaged, this caused the blood vessels to bleed. My lower left leg also sustained permanent nerve damage, along with a blood clot the size of a baseball bat.

That's not all the doctor found. My internal organs were squashed, as if I was a popped human water balloon. My spleen needed to be removed. My liver was lacerated and full of blood, my bladder torn open, and my diaphragm split to the extent that, combined with my injured lungs, I wouldn't be able to catch a deep breath for the next two years. The extent of my skull fracture, cracked at the basil section (or animalistic portion) would take more time to assess, but now they needed the bleeding to stop from my ears. All of this happened due to being flung through the air and landing with great force on the dirt road—followed by my SUV smashing on top of me before rolling off.

When I arrived at Palomar Pomerado, Mercy Air Life Flight performed a CRAMS (Circulation, Respiration, Abdomen, Motor, Speech) test on me. I scored a Zero. What did that mean? The answer was simple: I was toast, toes up, pushing daisies, never to see the light of day again. However, to Dr. Cloyd's amazement, I remained alive, fighting for my life. Never in Palomar Pomerado's fifty-year history had someone with such a low CRAMS rating survived. I set a hospital record—not necessarily the record I'd strived to achieve during college sports and my adult life. However, I remain damned glad to hold this record. I'm here, feet on the ground, head in the air, bodysurfing racing down waves instead of pushing up daisies, and living life fully. Yippy!

No one believed what they saw—a zero score for a *live* person. They didn't believe it throughout my first night, Dr. Cloyd among them. He, my family, as well as everyone else *hoped* I would survive the night; that was the extent of their outlook. I was out cold, and could not see or react to anything.

However, my sleeping body was filling up with a buzzing from prayers; they were warming my chest internally. I could hear them; there were so many! Who was saying these prayers? I didn't actually eavesdrop and hear every fine detail of each prayer, but I knew they were headed toward God for lil' ol' me!

Later, I learned all the prayers came from a packed high school stadium during the moment of silence at the football game, and then from all my friends in the visiting room, as well as many from the Palomar staff. Nurses do in fact pray for their charges who are in grave need, perhaps even for all of them. They are believers of Hebrews 11:1: "Now faith is the substance of things hoped for, the evidence of things not seen." I'm sure that, besides the obvious good deed toward the patient, praying helps them cope better with their daily duties and also creates some emotional distance from their patients. The spiritual life has that effect. Without prayer, or meditation, I can't see how nurses make it through all the dire situations that come through the hospital doors, mine among them. My view is that nurses are our angels here on earth.

My celestial travel guide, my Angel, returns. I'd been waiting for her since she took hold of me while I lay on Pauma Heights Road, and then left me in the meadow. Where had she gone? Would she come back? I felt myself growing frantic—not about surviving, but about seeing her and Heaven again.

Now she's back. *Thank you, God.*

We again travel upward, past the review meadow, zipping through an expanded tunnel. The sky is full of amazing clouds and brilliant rainbows, swirling prisms of color; the Angels above me and the colors are singing praises to God. Amazing . . .

This singing is the Omniscient feeling of Love. It has a particular sound: the Word, Amen, Aum, Om—the beginning of the Creation. It's captured perfectly in the very first verse of the Old Testament: "In the beginning was The Word, and The Word was with God." I become baptized or absorbed in the holy stream of the Divine Sound. My chest fills with the vibration of this constant caroling, a thunderous sound with a familiar tempo, like waves crashing on a beach. (Two years later at a Christmas service, the congregation was singing a song that had a repeat of "Hallelujah, Hallelujah, Hallelujah!" On the third Hallelujah, I felt a vibrating in my chest—the exact vibration as this caroling.) I look above and all around, trying to see the thousands upon thousands of Angels I can hear. I cannot see them, but I feel their love and their presence. It's as if they are above in a type of loft made of clouds—my Lord's choir room. Practice is taking place.

My Angel and I speed to a higher point; as fast as a blink we are catapulting at the speed of light, spiraling through a tunnel once again. We reach the highest point of an even deeper blue sky, which opens to a brilliant silvery white center. We reach this massive sphere of energy, the blinding white light that seems to engulf everything, like a pulsating quasar. Its power overwhelms me. I am in sheer awe and wonder fills my heart. My soul realizes it has come into the presence of the Absolute, and I now know God as only a Reality! How this touches my soul is beyond my understanding, but I know my soul absolutely recognized it before my mind would even consider the thought.

I lower my eyes from the blinding light. The sphere of God is racing through my mind. A sort of clearing of my thoughts is taking place. *What?* God is a man, I reason, not a sphere, or a light! As I realize, no name or gender can describe it. Nor can anything in the creation of darkness or light take away or deny the strength emanating from it. It's very similar to looking at the sun at high noon, except the sun is a yellow light, while this sphere is a brilliant white light—*and Divine!*

I knew this place, the heavy stuff "level," was a step above everything I'd experienced. Just then, without any prompting from me, my whole experience begins to appear in levels, so I can try to understand it better. The first step, or "level," was my Angel coming to me, offering peace and comfort as she traveled by my side while God embraced and cradled me in His arms. I jetted through the spiraling transparent tunnel, and then *whooshed* high into the sky.

The second step, or "level," was being placed on the ledge for my life's cause-and-effect review. I had to fully experience all the hatred, shame, fear, grief, condemnation, race prejudice, and pride of pedigree I'd expressed. Still I argued with my Angel that it was my time. I'd seen the candy store, I had the checklist of how I'd behaved, the chores I've completed and where my heart was when I completed them. I felt like a child standing with his/her father, trying desperately to earn allowance, except now I was trying desperately to earn His Glory. I wanted more, but after that review, I wasn't certain if I was worthy of any allowance or allowances.

The third step, or "level," was dancing in and among the Valley, certainly not the foreboding landscape of Psalms 23: "Lord, though I walk through the Valley of the Shadow of Death, I shall fear no evil." This valley lived. I was stunned by the perfection, the blending of each part of this world. Each particle and molecule had its own full life, and yet they were interconnected. Every cell or atom of this heavenscape emanated the highest praises toward the Creator of it all. Now this?

Then it dawned on me: *It is the same for us on earth.* Everything in our world is drawn-out in perfection, a mathematical symmetry not noticed with the naked eye. Ever look at the perfect diagram of a nautilus shell, a sunflower, a pinecone, or the mastery of the human body? What happens in all creation is governed by law— Natural Law or the Laws of Nature, the principles that operate the universe. Each phase in life prepares us for the next phase or level. Every moment and thing in is life is interconnected as a whole. While I'm thinking all of this a portion of the heavenscape became a waterfall, simply because my mind wished it. The flowers popped up for me to enjoy, unanticipated and unexpected circumstances, what we might call "miracles" in life.

I realized the larger, Biblical miracles were not recorded to astonish us or fill us with fear; instead, they provide examples of God's direct presence in the world. These things are revealed to me like a wake-up call: "God is present in the world, so Martha, get ready." This was all so interesting to me; these were not thoughts or knowledge I had prior. It was as if the knowledge of the world was being planted in my brain, so I would have a better understanding of the things I was seeing. When the verse "My father's house has many mansions" passed through me, I didn't see mansions of brick and mortar, but mansions of gold in Nature.

I've passed through these three "levels," wondering what could possibly add to this. Now I find out. My Angel with me again we zip past atoms into a deep sky that combines all the elements: gaseous, fiery, liquid, and solid. It reveals the cosmic beauty of the astral sky, not as we see it while looking up at a periwinkle or clear blue sky with a few clouds here and there, but infinite sky. It spreads out forever, full of color, each vision so pure and positive. This is very hard for me to describe; how is it that a sky and color is "positive"? Yet that's the energy and emotion that fills my soul.

The Angel swiftly moves down and below this sphere, to the right side of this light, this overwhelming power of divinity. She seems very humbled. Her reverence amazes me; I can feel her being fill with the utmost respect and honoring, and how she loves this brilliant divine light. This light is the strongest power I've ever felt. Then a magnificent beauty fills my senses with warmth and love, letting me know that everything in the physical and spiritual life is alive; every particle, every cell, every atom is filled with love.

My Angel quickly folds her wings on her back and kneels as if bowing; she is in prayer. Simultaneously, I am filled with both the deepest fear and the most intense feeling of love—more fear or love than I have ever felt.

Now I am to meet God, the Divine Agape Love, the Omnipresent Holy Spirit. *Um, The Holy Spirit . . . WOW . . .* is all I can think.

The door opens, metaphorically speaking (there are no doors), and I'm in deep meditation, gazing at the eternal sphere, its aura filled with electricity. It . . . He . . . has a magnetic draw. My heart becomes perfectly purified by this spiritual light of Universal Love. I am in the seat of Bliss. I can't friggin' believe it! *Really . . . me?*

I realize it in every inch of my six-foot body—it screams through my brain that this enormous white presence of energy is God and the Trinity, united as one. "Let there be light," "The Lord will be your everlasting Light . . . now this illuminating light is going to expose my truths." Talk about feeling like a little girl in church coming to a sudden awakening! I can almost hear my mother snapping her fingers to get me to sit up straight and pay attention.

As my being glows from all of this light and love, I recognize this is entirely different from the perception of Heaven I was given as a child. I was raised in the Episcopal Church, St. Michael's By the Sea, across the street from the beach in the Southern California coastal town of Carlsbad. On many Sundays, my larger focus was, quite simply, when do we go to the beach? Episcopalian beliefs and its formal traditions are similar to that of the Catholic Church. Thus, I had a sense that Heaven was a place, with buildings and streets of gold. However, now in this real Heaven, there are no buildings, castles, or homes, no streets of gold, or roads of any color. That was just one of many qualities and characteristics of Heaven that differed entirely from my beliefs.

I start shaking with awe. Deep within my heart, I think, "Uh-oh," the chill filling me. Not knowing what else to do, watching my Angel kneeling in prayer, I feel like a small child back at Saint Michaels on Easter morning, afraid if I'm not a good girl I won't get my Easter basket of goodies. I go on auto pilot and start reciting the Lord's Prayer: *Our Father who art in Heaven, hallowed be thy name, thy kingdom come, thy will be done, on Earth as it is in Heaven . . .* boy, did I hear those words loud and clear!

As this is happening, I keep focusing on the Trinity. I had never really given any thought to the idea; in my mind, the Father, Son, and Holy Ghost were three separate beings, not one form of totality. Somehow I pictured God as a massive, Herculean man with ultimate strength and power, the one to pass judgments on our life's quality or value. In other words, the Old Testament taskmaster we all grew up hearing about! I saw the Son, Jesus, as a sweet, nurturing man with a heart filled with love and kindness, with the spirit of a teacher. For me, the Holy Ghost ruled our feelings of guilt, shame, or pride like the babysitter of our thoughts, the keeper of our interior self.

I assume I acquired these views from art, as well as things I'd heard. I was raised in a family of teachers that valued history, art, and education most importantly. If you think about it, God is always portrayed as a stunning, strong, singular man who oversees everything and usually has a shine or glow around him. The Heavens shine behind him, and paintings of Jesus often include children and sheep, hence the kindly teacher. As for the Holy Ghost? Don't know of any pictures of that, but there is something about that word "ghost" that made me assume "keeper of thoughts" . . . you can't sneak anything past him, a ghost can pass right through you . . . Who knows how or why we come up with things we choose to believe? Now with it right in front of my face, I see them as they truly are, together as one, the Trinity, the Triune God.

This new (to me) all-encompassing God bestowed Love on all people and all things. This grew into what I now consider one of the greatest spiritual blessings of my taste of eternity, which I brought from Heaven into my new life. This overwhelming Love, incomprehensible as it might be to imagine, will engulf and hold me again when I return to Heaven! I'm blessed just knowing this. Also, I know the true essence of God is Love. I long to be filled with this complete, total Love.

While trying to comprehend the triune God, I also realize the nature of death. We fear death, we run away from it, we even demonize it, but would we continue to fear, run, or demonize if we really *knew* it? What it truly and ultimately signifies? A release from this world and a passing over into a true sanctuary for our souls? Heaven itself?

Another thing is happening, which takes place at the moment of my physical, clinically pronounced death: My energy has accelerated. I'm vibrating faster than before. My frequency has shifted. God threw a switch, and I began to *live* on another wavelength. If you think of life in terms of a network, this increase in frequency is comparable to living our physical lives on AM radio, without Wi-Fi. When we have peak experiences that make us feel most alive—jumping off cliffs, falling in love, hitting a grand slam, visiting a dreamed-about destination for the first time, having big-time prayers answered—our frequency shifts to the equivalent of Wi-Fi. We're more aware, more alive, our senses heightened, all systems go, our minds more clear and focused. I think of it as being in the zone, being more alive . . . but I know that it's also drawing me closer to the frequencies present in Heaven!

When we die, that frequency shifts again to a sort of satellite radio Wi-Fi broadcasting every conceivable station at warp-speed. This higher wavelength fills every cell of us with an even greater *life*. Our body remains at the same spot on the dial, but our awareness, our soul intensifies a few notches. It is our *consciousness*, our soul, that shifts.

That is all that death entails . . . a shift. *Life* awaits us in Heaven. We don't die in the way we picture the word; we aren't extinguished. The original texts of every major religion and spiritual path say the same thing when it comes to this. They speak of eternal life or everlasting life. It's not only about parking our souls in Heaven; there's more to it than that. Isn't that wonderful?

After the accident, I spent a dozen years searching for this understanding of death and life in my studies, and did not find the answers. Then one day, I saw my experience of "energy" described for the first time in *The Holy Science*, a small but potent book written in 1894 by Sri Yukteswar, a learned scientist, sage, and mentor in India. In this book, he quotes Jesus Christ's scriptures as the way to live life. This book also quotes Jesus' descriptions of light, specifically John 1:9: "*That was the true Light, which lighteth every man that cometh into the world.*"

Seeing that life is in every cell, in every particle of every-thing, filled with its own quality of light, sound, and frequency, each being a component of light, I finally felt validation of my new personal understanding of life and God—the understanding I was shown in Heaven. God is Love and he is part and parcel of everyone and everything. Truly, the Kingdom of Heaven is within you and me!

After being immersed in this love and magnificent beauty, hearing the beautiful sounds, feeling the warmth, and smelling the incredible fragrance that filled my etheric senses, I no longer struggle with fear of death. I truly have no fear of it at all. To be truthful, I can't wait; I long to be embraced with such love again.

There is one more bit of remaining "business" in my meeting with the Almighty. While I was on the ledge, I argued with my Angel about it being my time. Even though she left while I had my review, I still argued it was indeed my time. In the Valley, I danced and frolicked in complete freedom, mesmerized and en-joying the valley of death. That made me certain it was my time! How could it not be? I never wanted to leave.

Once again I'm told it's not my time. This time I know it's the Trinity that tells me this. Now, I'm scared beyond belief, but still I'm being filled with total love. The assertive side of me takes over (traits and characteristics magnify in Heaven, just like the entire consciousness). I have the audacity to beg God directly to let me stay . . . and do I ever beg!

Soon, I sense his bemusement with me. He studies my life review on a type of transparent screen, which I would now com-pare somewhat to the invisible boards where data or pictures are projected, like you might see on episodes of *NCIS*, *Star Trek*, or *Scorpions*. He watches it all, complete with sound, touch, taste, and smell as the component parts of me, of who I am. Except he gets the full screening, with no edits or outtakes lying on the floor. There I am: the good, the bad, and the ugly. *Again.*

The Divine asks why I feel it is my time. I answer like a petulant first grader, "'Cause I want to stay here."

He makes a deal with me. He assures me I have free will, but he then deploys a parental reverse psychology. Via a telepathic wavelength of some kind, he shows me that I have been a good parent, that my boys love me. And then he implants in my soul, "I will show you what will happen to your boys if you return, and then I will show you what will happen to them if you stay. Then We will make your decision."

Fair enough. My mind starts dancing. *I've got it! I'm staying!* My mind twirling like a two-year-old, *I'm gonna stay in Heaven!*

But what he showed me gave me a far different outlook.

Waking & the Veil of Heaven

I never heard any of the rush or bustle of the ER room.

Amazing . . . He'd just spent eight hours on his feet, performing one of the busiest and most stressful surgeries he would experience. Following an evening and late night like this, most doctors would have washed up and headed home for a deep sleep. Not Dr. Cloyd. He sat in the chair next to my bed, guarding me like a warrior, calmly watching and monitoring my vitals as my family walked in for another reason . . . *to say good-bye.*

Despite his optimistic attitude, Dr. Cloyd wasn't sure I'd make it through the night. Later, I learned Dr. Cloyd never relinquished the chair to a family member, nor anyone else. He remained at my side all night long. As far as I'm concerned, this medical warrior became a saint and savior that night, a side of him not seen or appreciated enough. I certainly appreciated it.

Meanwhile, my boys stayed up all night, not knowing my condition . . . or if they'd ever see me again. They came in to say good-bye, just in case I didn't make it through the night. Nathan didn't recognize me: "Mom, your head was so swollen, it was the size of a basketball," he told me later. Can you imagine looking at your mother, not recognizing her, and not knowing if you will ever get her back? And, even if she survived, not knowing what shape or mental capacity she would possess after all the injuries and brain damage?

Unfortunately, Nate and Aaron lived with this reality for several years, the time it took me to slowly regain my physical and mental faculties, and to again become their active, lively, strong mother. Of course, along with that came the woman who was never afraid of speaking her mind—for better or worse! I'm sure they would have appreciated *that* less, but it's another story for another day.

After the boys said their final good-byes, the waiting began. My parents, brothers, and sister gathered into the immediate family waiting room. It was dark, "a room I didn't want to be in, Mom," Aaron said. The agitation lingers with him to this day. He and Nate, along with a few of their closest friends, sat on the cold tile floor . . . waiting. Everyone who has visited a loved one fighting for life knows the feeling. The mud-thick atmosphere in the room that smells of old coffee and antiseptic, hands and hearts gnash as you continually say to yourself, "She's still alive, she's still alive," while hoping you get to repeat that for the next forty years or so.

Because of my skull fracture, crushed internal organs, and numerous broken bones, Dr. Cloyd decided to put me in a medically induced coma, at the time a new procedure. Not all doctors would have known to do it. It was sort of like packing my brain on ice to stop the swelling and delay or offset the expected mental damage. While others openly discussed the possibility I would be brain dead or in a somewhat vegetative state, he was not convinced. He guided one of my family members through a list of simple commands for me. Dr. Cloyd figured I would be more likely to respond if the command came from a voice I recognized.

Then came the voice: "Raise your right arm."

I did. *Good.*

"Now raise your left arm . . . no, your other left arm."

Up went my left arm. Done.

Not quite. "Okay now focus, Martha. I need you to raise your right leg . . . good. Now, raise your left leg . . . come on, give it all you've got. You can do it. Raise your left leg."

I could only lift my leg an inch off the table. I'd injured it too badly when it was pinned beneath my body.

The plan was to take stress out of the healing process. The coma would make it easier for me to lay still and heal. A metal belt was placed around my broken hip to hold it in place, and I was placed in a rotating bed, designed to add motion to aid in reducing bedsores and frozen joints, and enhance circulation.

Dr. Cloyd didn't set out further instructions. He only said the recovery would be long and challenging, mentally and physically. His big question: How much memory would I lose, both short- and long-term? My short-term memory would be the most affected . . . a good thing, since it would reduce the stress of re-living the accident. When they lifted me out of the coma, then they would know more, he added.

That early conversation eased my husband's pain, knowing that the doctor also believed I would not be a vegetable. Any further mental issues would be addressed later, things such as how I'd be able to process information, communicate, and retain information.

Dr. Cloyd turned to one of the nurses. "Okay, put her out." With that, the coma was induced.

Meanwhile, the attending physicians started talking about the likelihood I had sustained irreversible brain damage, which only heated up Dr. Cloyd. "The only people who seem to know she's not brain dead are me, the nurse, and her husband," he told everyone in the room.

God's reveal was too much for my soul to take. I was shown that if I did not return, my boys would turn down the wrong road. I saw they would be told they were perfect in everything they did, and this would make them feel entitled, like they could do no wrong. This is not a good thing for a young mind. I believe a parent is there to guide and help mold their kids, not be their friends (until later, when they are adults).

The reveal didn't stop there. I was also shown that my boys, being raised primarily by their grandmother, would end up ruling over her, not appreciating her for her love. They would not have a male role model to follow. They would be separated from my family, where my three brothers were fine examples of manhood, different from each other but equally strong role models. Then my boys would end up making all the wrong choices.

Aaron would be dumped by his girlfriend, dive into drugs, hard-core music a wasted life with all the judgments that would come along with it. He would follow his friends into a trashy life. He had wanted to dye his hair when he was younger and I used to say to him jokingly, "If it's a color that can be found on a natural head of hair, then you can dye yours that color. If not, then no. If you want to live here, there will be no ink, no piercings. Why would you want to mark up such a stunning body? You might hate me now for this, but later, you just might thank me. That's a risk I'm willing to take."

Make that *half*-jokingly. I wasn't strict, but I directed my boys firmly, often using humor to deliver the message. You know the immortal *Mary Poppins* lyric, "Just a spoonful of sugar helps the medicine go down"? That was my philosophy.

Nate, instead of joining a church and following in his faith, would end up angry with God, forsake him, and lose his faith altogether. He would have grave difficulty and would drop out of high school. Too many negative influences would overwhelm and dictate the course of my sons' decisions.

Little did I know what ugly twists and turns lives can take due to the loss of a parent. The trickle-down effect was beginning to present itself to me. These scenarios were so frightening that I don't even like to think of them now, fifteen years later. I don't know of anything stronger than a mother's protective nature when it comes to her offspring. After viewing this in Heaven, one feeling raced through my soul: *Get back there, get back now . . . and protect them.*

As free will works on earth, so it works in Heaven. It all comes down to the choices we make. Which leads to the next segment of God's reveal: choices. The Divine gave me a preview of my future and my boys, of what would happen if I returned to my life. I was shown life would change, not be as smooth, not as upscale, harder in many ways for me. My boys would still enjoy a nice life, make good choices, and become good, responsible men loyal to their women, their jobs, and their greater purposes (which is exactly what has happened).

I knew instantly! I would gladly take what came to me, anything that would spare my sons the horrific parallel reality I saw. The Divine also showed me scenarios that were disturbing in their own right. Sadly, they came to pass, and my friends wondered how I handled them so well (it helps if you see the preview first). I saw my marriage coming to an end, denigrated by a number of things I could not then stand, or most importantly with love, forgive (divorce happened five years after my accident). In 2014, my girlfriend, Cindy Weaver, told me I was one of the strongest women she knew, and how much she respected the way I've dealt with so many trials. The Weave, as I like to call Cindy, didn't know that none of the trials were new to me; I'd had previews of them in Heaven. That's not to say it's any easier to be mocked as you learn to walk and talk again by your special someone, even if they say the doctors insisted they should guide me with tough love. Because of that, I was better prepared and steadier for future storms.

I was shown in my preview that I would need to find a job after being a stay-at-home mom for seventeen years. Getting a job in my forties? With no college degree? That was daunting! However, I always found my comfort and interest in homes. I had been a property appraiser in Coeur d'Alene, Idaho, in my twenties. I loved decorating, I knew a fair bit about mortgages, and I raised my sons in a stable, centered home. Therefore, I knew my job would have something to do with this. I was shown I would then lose my job—twice—and then I would lose my home. Even though I knew I would lose my home it still wasn't easy to accept.

I was shown I would search for myself while struggling with the confusion of not feeling that I belong anywhere, that I'd share all of what I had seen in Heaven with others. I saw I would hide and ignore truths, and this would only cause me more pain. I also saw that my understanding of religion and search for faith would expand greatly and embrace the points in common of all religions . . . and I would lose friends along the way.

There was one other thing God showed me, plain as day: this book. From the moment I awoke from my coma, I knew the title. *It's not "near-death," but a "Taste of Eternity,"* my soul whispered persistently. I promised God (or rather begged) that if he allowed me to return to my babies, my boys, I would tell all! I would share His Love, Power, and Beauty. For months after I awoke, the phrase "a taste of eternity" passed through my dreams and thoughts. It drove me a little crazy, because I didn't understand what it meant.

I remained in the drug-induced coma for seven weeks. I remember specific moments of being afraid, and my Angel would appear and comfort me. She'd always appear to my right; looking at her was like viewing her through a windowpane, through a heavenly veil. She said nothing, but her presence was comfort enough.

As I lay in the coma, I could smell *everything,* which confirms for me what they say about the sense of smell, or the olfactory sense: It's the most primal of our five senses, the one most closely tied to our survival as human beings. And it's the last to leave us. It also confirmed what I'd heard about people when they grow blind or become deaf; their other senses compensate for those lost. My sense of smell took over, while the others idled in a form of cruise control like a hibernating animal. The common belief is that a comatose person is nearly as unaware as a stone. Not the case at all.

I could tell when someone entered the room. How? I smelled them. You know how babies carry a certain scent, like the incredibly fresh smell of their hair? Like practically every other mother I know, I remember smelling my babies' heads all the time when they were little. Likewise, I could tell one visitor in my room from another by their smell; this filled me with peace. Unfortunately, I remember one nurse that wasn't very smooth or gentle administering IVs and medicine with needles. Whenever she entered my room, I braced to feel the pain of the needle in my arm. While I winced inside all she saw was a woman resting peacefully in a coma.

My husband's voice and smell were always calm and present. I later found out he talked softly into my ear. By doing so, he calmed me down whenever one or more of the many machines lit up or beeped with their alarms. After that, the machines would settle down and give the accurate readings my doctors needed.

During this time, the doctors told my family something they and Dr. Cloyd had refused to acknowledge: Due to my brain swelling and the basal cortex skull fracture, I would more than likely be a mental vegetable. This might manifest as animal reactions like growling or flashes of extreme anger. When I was transferred to the UC-San Diego Medical Center for hip replacement surgery (which never happened), the doctors advised my family to look into assisted care.

My husband didn't buy it. He had seen my direct response when he asked me to raise my arms and legs after the surgery. I'd even raised the wrong arm, and when he asked me to raise the correct one, I'd done it. He had heard Dr. Cloyd's comment about how huge it was that I could respond to his requests. I can imagine, with a big smile on my face, what might have gone through his mind: *You haven't been around this woman when someone tells her she can't do something!*

My sister and mom reacted far differently. They checked out where to best place me, or how to find the best home care. Katie checked information online, a new form of researching at the time, and she and mom both took classes offered by Scripps La Jolla Hospital on how to care for a vegetative family member. It frightened them that they may have to care for me; fearing others wouldn't be there for me if it came to that, they wanted to be educated. Best to be prepared for anything.

Meanwhile, I slept peacefully, quietly healing and enjoying short visits from my Guardian Angel. She always seemed to be there when these frightful discussions and feelings took place.

How do I know? My mother had a tendency to talk right over the top of me. I vividly remember her telling a visitor, "You know, they say she is going to be a complete vegetable, and more than likely live in a wheelchair." Inside, I screamed *NO! I'm right here! I'm going to be fine. Give me a chance!* How did I know it was her? By her scent.

Right there, at my side, was my Guardian Angel.

At night, I started "searching" for my husband, trying to locate his foot to lock mine around his. We normally slept this way, not touching except for winding our feet around each other's. I kept searching. I'd find the bed pole of the sides they lifted to lock me into the bed, and I'd cling onto it with my foot, hoping to be touching his. The nurse kept trying to make my foot stay up on the mattress. "Be a good girl," she told her comatose patient, "and keep your foot up, where it will be more comfortable."

Sometimes comments dropped to a level even more infantile. Some doctors and nurses think people in comas don't or can't hear anything. I heard a lot. This nurse even went to the length of tying my ankle to the bedpost. I specifically remember her request, the beeps of the machines, and the sound of my mother's voice as she talked to me.

In most ways, the medically induced coma shut me down completely. I saw black, as if my eyelids wouldn't open. I no longer felt the words in every cell and pore of my body, heart, and soul, as I had in Eternity. I only heard them. My heart wanted to break. I longed to feel the words. Part of that sense of loss came from my soul's new awakening to a God that I experienced first-hand. However, that did not resolve my innermost dilemma: *How do I keep what I experienced in Eternity with me on earth?* After returning to the world of physical consciousness, I found it difficult not seeing that love expressed in each and every person. I wanted it to stay with me forever.

I was transferred to UCSD Medical Center to undergo hip transplant surgery. While there, I developed pneumonia, and became too ill to have the surgery. My husband felt I wasn't getting the care I needed, and it was far more difficult for my family and friends to visit me. He knew their visits enhanced my chance of a strong recovery. He asked that I be transferred, but no such luck: This was a teaching hospital, and I had fantastic insurance. It was not going to be an easy request to fill.

Finally, my family members had enough. One walked in and said, "You either get her released and an ambulance to take her back to Palomar Hospital, or I'll carry her out of here and drive her myself." They wanted me to be in the hospital whose staff fought to save my life. "If you're not gonna do the hip surgery, then she needs to be close to family."

I spent the remainder of my coma in Palomar.

My mother was an avid reader, as well as a retired educator. While visiting me one day, she described the Farmers Market in downtown Escondido as if she were viewing it out my window. Mom, or Mumzie as I called her, knew I was familiar with the market and sometimes shopped for fruit and vegetables there, so she wisely used it to form the basis of her story. Truth be told, she couldn't see the streets below the hospital room at all, but she had driven past the farmer's market scene several times en route to visiting me. She described the kids and balloons, pumpkins carved into jack-o'-lanterns (it was Halloween season), deep-red tomatoes, fresh, sweet-smelling oranges, strong, pungent mushrooms, and lovely flower arrangements, her favorite being the bright yellow sunflowers.

Years later, when I shared my memory of her Farmer's Market story with her, she started to cry. She told me it had really been a rainy day and she was getting cabin fever in the room, so she thought of me as her little six-year-old girl and told me a story to keep my mind busy and my heart full.

I'm pretty sure, to this day, that I blew her away by recounting her story.

My family visited almost daily. What do you talk about to a comatose person? Well, we, the Brookhart family, can find some fun in everything. Knowing I would want music without words—this was my style—my hubby delivered CDs galore. Katie followed suit and bought a just-the-tunes Beatles CD. One day, while she and my brother Tim visited, they started singing along to the Beatles CD in a goofy attempt to entertain me (and themselves). My very own private concert! Years later, I heard my sister sing the same song; damned if it didn't all come rolling back to me. I mean, if you hear the Beatles sung in her *not* pitch-perfect voice, you're going to remember, even if locked in a coma.

My sister often took it upon herself to be my personal cosmetologist. On the day of my accident, I had my toenails painted (something I didn't do often). During the time I lay comatose, she stripped and painted my toenails, tweezed any wild hairs that needed it, and made lotion available to any visitor to rub on my feet and hands. Mary Kay had nothing on Katie as she tried to keep me in model form.

Finally, the big day arrived. As doctors started to lift me out of the coma, I wouldn't open my eyes. I could tell who was there without opening them, by their scent . . . my mom and dad, Katie, my brother Tim, his wife, Tini, and someone I didn't recognize. Later, I discovered it was my sister-in-law, Teri. They feared I would emerge in a persistent vegetative state, and were eager for me to wake up.

The people I'd been anticipating hadn't arrived . . . so I waited, eyes closed. Then the final arrival of my boys—I felt them. I *knew* they were in the corridor before they entered the room. I could feel their vibration and smell their distinct scents. I rolled my head, opened my eyes . . . and *there they were.* I started softly blowing gentle kisses to them, something I had done all their life. Odd . . . I was blowing kisses to an eleven- and fourteen-year-old? I knew who they were but . . . in my mind they were six and nine . . . my head injury had bumped me back about five years. However, in front of me was the *Why* and the *Reason* I had come back from Eternity.

I tried to speak, but no go, due to the tracheotomy tube in my throat. However, I had a pressing concern and needed an answer—now. I managed to ask for a pad of paper and pen. I desperately scribbled away, but I was too weak and mentally foggy. It was no use. Next I tried drawing; after all, I'd been a good artist. That was gone as well. I scratched out a picture that, to me, was clear: a building, a van, and a person. However, to all those present, my scribbling wasn't so obvious. They started a round of charades, trying to figure out my picture. I grew agitated . . . a good sign. It took them awhile to figure out that all I wanted to know was if Nate was in the car with me on the day of the accident, and how he got home. Always the mom . . . It was a cool moment for everyone when they figured it out. Most of all, they saw that I could communicate quite coherently.

Martha's vegetable aisle was officially closed for business.

When I awoke, my cloak for the past seven weeks, the Veil of Heaven, closed.

My world seemed amplified. I was hypersensitive to everything around me. I felt so disoriented; I wanted to go back to that totally loving God, the one that accepted all, back to the cradling warmth of Heaven. The good things seemed to feel so much better, but the bad things—like lying broken on a hospital bed—seemed so much worse. My first moments and hours of consciousness felt very strange. The fact I'd been comatose made my senses too sharp. I noticed every movement, every sound, and every change in room temperature.

I also felt invaded, beaten down by the TV. Reality seemed a grotesque matinee of a carnival spook house. How I wept deep inside when I heard the news—or worse, if a visitor watched a daytime program. It felt like I was watching a horror movie, with all of the world's ugliness pouring through the airwaves, ready to reach out and engulf me. Some of this had to do with the morphine dripping into my veins, but most of all, it was a matter of dipping the heavenly purity into the gutter. I buzzed the nurse again and again. Finally, she put a sign on the TV to leave it off because it distressed me so much.

Later that day—or was it the next?—my dad came to see me. I was so . . . happy to see him. *Daddy!* I had just left the loving arms of my Divine Father and felt secure having my earthly father with me. Forget about the fact I was forty. I was a little girl in distress, and my daddy was there to protect me.

I decided that he and my mother needed to know. I tried to communicate the beauty of what I experienced in Heaven, but the ventilator kept getting in my way. I was so excited . . . I had to let them know. All Mom and Dad understood was, "I went to the light." He smiled and wept. He knew exactly what I was trying to tell him.

During my coma, my family read to me and made sure we listened to music. My husband had gone to the effort to find CDs with the sounds of nature, birds, and the ocean. However, someone kept switching out my tunes and playing a country music CD. It sounded like a sad, wailing woman; I hated it. After I came out of the coma, whenever I awoke from sleeping, I'd buzz for the nurse. Despite my inability to talk, write, or move, I told her through my eyes that I needed that sound to stop. *Now!* I wanted that wailing woman out of my room. I found it difficult to see and hear things that didn't reflect love being expressed. I wanted it in all people.

I still do. In Eternity, this feeling of Love for all people and things is absolute, undeniable, a feeling unlike any other . . . and I wanted to get back!

ICU visits were supposedly limited to immediate family. However, Palomar Pomerado conveyed a caring, small-town attitude that extended the definition of "family." They turned the other way when Rob and Robin Gilster came into my room to visit. Rob and I would always have a special connection; he'd prayed over me immediately after the accident, calling in God. During their visit, I worked my hardest to be a proper socialite, even trying to introduce them to my parents, sister, and nurses despite an open tracheotomy. Everyone laughed and suggested I rest.

One of my biggest joys came about a week later. My baby Nate (I still call him that, even though he's six-foot-seven and in his mid-twenties) wanted to read my many get-well cards to me. When he was young, at the end of each day we would lie in bed and I'd read him bedtime stories. Now a big guy in junior high, he wanted to reprise our moment. This was great by me, because in my mind he was still my sweet six-year-old. My mother-in-law was afraid he would hurt my broken pelvis and hips, but we ignored her.

Nate snuggled into the bed gently. He lay very still while he read each card aloud. Tears of joy streaked down our cheeks. I can still see the look in Nate's eyes as he first saw me after I woke up: *Looks like Mom, but doesn't walk, talk, or act like Mom . . . Hmmmm . . .*

That's quite a lot for any eleven-year-old.

I sized myself up. *Ouch.* I had lost nearly fifty pounds. Every muscle in my body had atrophied, which hurt even more because I had prided myself on being a tomboy as a child, and then a very fit athlete as an adult. I had been a strong, physically fit woman who excelled at tennis and golf, played on softball teams, ran with her sons, and wasn't afraid to climb mountains or jump off cliffs (as those who were with me in India on my fifty-third birthday know, I'm still not afraid to jump off cliffs!).

Now, my immediate challenge was to simply lift my head. I looked the same, but I wasn't the same. My brain injury and ensuing coma slowed down my mind. I felt very foggy, lost in some ways. I hated it when the nurse washed my hair in a little spittoon. It was curved so it could fit under either the patient's head or chin. She scrubbed away, her fingernails digging into my skull, and she was not rinsing all the shampoo out. It drove me crazy to know the soap scum sat in my hair, but despite that, I was happy just to have it washed. Drugs give you a greasy head . . . in more ways than one. The worst was the miniature man's comb. I have thick, long hair like a horse's mane. My day nurse would rack that comb through my hair, tearing it out as she went. To my mom, a teacher, it had the agonizing effect of fingers on a chalkboard.

Thankfully, Mumzie was there. One day after washing my hair, the nurse grew tired of fighting to get the tangles out of my hair. She decided to cut it off. Mumzie entered the room as the nurse made her first cut, to my bangs. "What are you doing?" Mom cried out.

They began to argue. "You're not doing your daughter any favors by insisting she keep her hair," the nurse said. "Her condition is going to be long and drawn out, and it will be easier on her if we just cut it all off."

"Absolutely not!" Mom barked. Her bark was as tough as any dog's bite. Or mama bear's, for that matter. As for Mom's bite? The nurse quickly got a taste: "Martha's hair is part of her, part of who she is, always has been and always will be! You cut it off, and I'll go to your board."

The nurse thought my mom was in denial over what she would need to confront sooner or later: that I would be a mental vegetable. That didn't matter; no way Mom would let that nurse cut off my hair.

My hair stayed on my head. Thank God she was there; it may have been harder for me to bounce back under a shiny dome. Perhaps there is a little of Samson in me; after all, he told Delilah he would lose his strength if he lost his hair.

As much as my mom understood the importance I placed on my hair, she didn't yet realize how badly my skull had been injured. I could feel the searing pain across the back of my skull when she held my head down. I also saw the looks of pity on my family members' faces as they treated me like a baby.

One afternoon, despite my drugged-out, fazed-out brain, I wanted to prove I was strong. I would do everything for myself. I tried desperately to raise my head off the pillow, even if only a few inches. I watched in horror as Mom bolted across the room, her maternal instincts in overdrive. "No, no . . . you sit still!" Then a sledgehammer slammed my head back down . . . only it was her hand. She'd merely put her palm firmly across my forehead and pushed me to the pillow. She was so afraid I would hurt something, pull something out, or cause a broken bone to unset.

During this first week of consciousness, whenever a nurse would leave my wrists free from their bedpost straps, I tried to pull out all the feeding and sedation tubs. I even tried to lift my legs over the side rails, thinking I would just walk out of the hospital.

You can't keep me in a cage, people! What I didn't understand was that I couldn't even sit up, much less stand or climb out of the bed. I wouldn't be walking out of the hospital. Yet, I kept plotting . . . one of my favorite little memories.

It wasn't all bad. A wonderful scent of lavender was always accompanied by soothing rubs up and down my arms, with soft hands floating across my cheeks. Katie would hand the lotion bottle to whomever arrived, and they would get the "honor" of rubbing it on my feet, arms, hands, and cheeks. It was also a nice distraction for them. While I enjoyed the free massages, they could focus on something besides how much body fat I'd lost, my atrophied muscles, or my mental state. I never forgot the lotion.

A decade later, the lotion bottle went into the other hand when my mother was in the last few weeks of her life. Since I was on a leave of absence from work after having uterine cancer surgery, I could visit Mumzie every day. I gave her massages on her feet, hands, and forehead with a lavender-infused lotion. I talked to her in a soft voice and let her know how much I loved her, and how her strength, though sometimes hard to accept, was one of the qualities that helped give me the strength of will I carry today. As I rubbed her feet, her eyes rolled back in her head in complete pleasure.

A few years later, in 2014, I brought out the lotion again. My Pauma Valley bestie, MaryAnn Borden, was dying. I hadn't kept in close touch with her for three years; we chatted on the phone but she never mentioned anything about illness. She was the happy sort, so I had no idea she was so close, so near death. A friend called me, knowing that I would want to be told. "Can I visit her?" I asked. "Is there any way?"

"Yes, tomorrow would be good."

I immediately knew what I wanted. I ran to the store and bought the best lavender lotion I could find. MaryAnn had a second home in Idaho, and she would often bring me back wild lavender lotion. We once spent a winter husking and rolling the lavender she grew on her property.

When I arrived, I gave her husband, Steve, a big hug. "It's too bad it takes something like this to bring people together," he said. *Ugh,* that rang true.

The hospice caregiver took me to MaryAnn. The hospice lady was speaking to me in a low tone, letting me know how critical MaryAnn was. With that, MaryAnn opened her eyes, smiled one of her big smiles, and said, "Martha and I have been here before, only the last time, it was her that was going."

For the next forty-five minutes, MaryAnn was alert, thrilled and deeply pleasured as I rubbed her feet, arms, and face. We talked about our lives, our boys, and how they are what both of us live for She told me about her younger son Mattie's wedding, how much she loved his wife, and how her older son Chase was such a hard worker. She added how good they were to her, and tried to show me a necklace they had given her the week prior.

Then MaryAnn asked me about Heaven and the Angels. I rubbed her feet while trying to hold back my tears, knowing my girl was about to enter that Bliss, that awesome Love. This woman could buy anything she desired, which had never made me jealous, but this was a different story. She had already started to cross through the veil, and I envied her. I watched her several times as she drifted out of consciousness and her face lit up with awe. My mom did the same at her point of death. They both had received a little Taste of Eternity. After sharing a few things with MaryAnn, mostly the love and beauty that pervades in Heaven, I could tell she was failing; it was time to let her sleep so I left.

The next day, MaryAnn passed.

The doctors came into my room with news: I would be transferred to a rehabilitation hospital in San Diego. My next step? Learning how to use a wheelchair.

That goal sounded way too low for me. I already had something else in mind: to walk again.

Chapter 7

Hospital Caregivers

Shortly after I emerged from my seven-week coma, I was transferred from Palomar Pomerado to Scripps Hospital's rehabilitation
wing in San Diego. My biggest objective, as far as doctors and
my family were concerned? Learning how to use a wheelchair.
Based on my condition, my best case prognosis, my loved ones
hoped my mental faculties would fully return enough for me to
learn how to live in and operate a wheelchair.

My expectations were a little higher. Make that a lot higher: I
wanted to walk again and to return to my place as a mother. One
can always hope for miracles, right?

As they readied me for the ambulance ride, I was like a little two-year-old girl. The only person with me was my mom. I
wanted her to ride in the ambulance with me. She was more than
willing . . . but she needed someone to pick her up from Scripps.
Who would that be on a weekday morning? Scripps was more than
an hour's drive from Carlsbad, and my dad wasn't feeling well
enough. Nor was Mom, for that matter. She watched helplessly
as the EMT maneuvered her youngest child as though I were a
hopeless, useless piece of meat, not the physically vital and athletically competitive forty-year-old she knew before the accident.

They loaded me up and strapped me down in the back of the
ambulance. What a rush—I was so frightened to be in a vehicle of
any kind. And it was so cramped. Neighbors in Pauma Valley sent

me a soft stuffed animal, a little cocker spaniel. My mom placed him in my arms before they wheeled me down the corridor to the ambulance, trying to stop me from crying. I was petrified. Little did I know that this cute little plush animal would become such a great companion. I named him Sandy Dog, after a toy Aaron owned when he was four.

As the ambulance wove its way down the freeway, Sandy Dog and I snuggled tight, my tears running all over his fur. The medic talked to me, letting me know that everyone at the new hospital would be so nice and kind. I had nothing to worry about, he said. When we arrived, the EMTs gently lifted me off the transport gurney and into the bed, my new medic friend sweetly placing Sandy Dog under the covers in the crook of my right arm. He knew I suffered from a frozen shoulder and considerable tissue damage in that arm. He even kissed my forehead. "You're gonna do great here, and your mom and family will be here soon," he said. He and others delivered me to my room.

On that first day, I was still not talking, because my neck hadn't yet closed from the tracheotomy; they'd only removed it a few days prior. My check-in nurse entered the room, and promptly told me to stop crying. "You're fine!" she snapped. She was a middle-aged, hardened lady, perhaps an ex-military nurse. She had no patience at all. I was simply a new charge for her, a new addition to her routine. She started shifting me all about, apparently not liking the way the EMTs had placed me in the bed. She yanked on the sheets, and then flipped me by my feet from one side to the other, rolling my hips. I moaned and screeched loudly from the searing pain. Again she told me I was fine, that she wasn't hurting me. I held my fingers to my neck, blocked the tracheotomy hole, and yelled, "I broke my hips; you're hurting me!" "Read my chart!" It came out as a rasp.

She grabbed my chart and glanced over it. Her eyes widened. "You've been through it, haven't you?" She immediately softened and became kinder. She asked what I remembered from my accident. "I have seen an Angel," I told her.

She walked up to my face, firmly gripped my shriveled bicep, and stared into my eyes. "Never tell anyone what you just said, or they'll never let you out of here." She made it sound like something negative, like there was no place for God in this life.

I was so let down, demoralized, and depressed, which I had never been in my life. This space was so different from the beauty of Heaven, from the kindness of the ICU and step-down care of Palomar Hospital. I lay there alone, feeling like a frightened child, afraid I would never receive a family visit. I wanted to scream at her, "I did see an Angel! There is a Heaven, and it's full of love and kindness!" I didn't talk much to her or the other nurses that came in my room. Instead, I tried to embrace the feeling of love that wrapped me in Heaven—and Palomar Pomerado Hospital, for that matter.

The next morning, I was fitted for a wheelchair, my new legs. They wheeled me to the main physical therapy room and introduced me to my home and new job for the next month. Out of the many therapists, I was assigned the one whose grandparents lived in my town. Julie West was a twenty-something, an athletic stud of a girl, with a brain, compassion, and belief in God. I sensed that right away . . . even though neither she nor I had mentioned God. She visited her grandparents often in Valley Center, and could relate to the rural small town feeling I described to her during our endless days of training my ragdoll body to perform correctly. She was great and we truly enjoyed each other's company, even though the therapy was painful. Providence or coincidence? Why was she the one chosen to be my therapist?

Julie wheeled me about, showing me the rooms in which we would be working: the weight room, kitchen—and The Room. The torture room. Stretching tables the size of queen-size beds filled the room, the tables upholstered in vinyl, the perfect height of a wheelchair. And then there were the parallel bars. Wasn't that an apparatus gymnasts used? What was it doing in a rehabilitation center?

Julie outlined the plan. I sat in my chair thinking, *Yeah right, I'm sure I'm gonna be able to do all that. Right. Keep dreaming.* Julie excused herself to speak with another therapist, leaving me to watch a lady at the parallel bars. I watched in horror as a lady tried to walk. Holding herself between the bars, she slowly shuffled one leg and then the other, moving her hands along the bars once her leg was in place. She managed three steps before starting to lose her balance. Her physical therapist talked to someone else, not watching her.

As I watched this whole thing go down and saw her slipping, I wanted to call out to get someone's attention—anyone's—but my voice had no projection. The words wouldn't come out. She started to fall. I wanted to jump up to her aid, but I couldn't even kick to get anyone's attention. She crashed to the ground, mortifying her therapist, who suddenly started paying attention again.

Julie raced quickly to my side. Suddenly nauseous, my body stiffened and became riddled with pain. Julie took me back to my room, explaining how these things never happen. Funny . . . I just saw it happen! She administered my morphine drip, which would become a very good friend of mine for the next several months.

The next morning, Julie greeted me in my room. She sat me up and dressed me, a daily routine that would bring us closer each day. We suited up and headed back to the main room. I saw the lady from the parallel bars. She wore a cast on her arm; she had broken it in her fall. Fear paralyzed me—and I'm not the breed of girl who fears much, roller coasters and joyrides at even one hundred miles per hour . . . ? Hum . . . I'm in for a thrill every time. But now . . . I was beyond scared.

"We will move along slowly, and I will never leave you," Julie said. "We'll only work to the point of pain that you can handle." She patted my shoulder. "But there surely will be pain," she added.

Pain didn't bother me. Falling and breaking my arm while my therapist wasn't there to spot me did.

Meanwhile, the lady with the cast stood up to the parallel bars, a new therapist by her side, and forced her legs to move, one after the other. I looked up at Julie. "No pain no gain"; that's all I could manage to say. What I thought was, *If that lady can do this after breaking her arm, then so can I.* I was an athlete for a reason. I've never been a quitter; I wasn't about to quit now, and my boys needed me. After all, that's why I came back from Heaven.

Julie placed me on the mat, and slowly started stretching my arms and legs, rolling me from side to side. With each stretch, my brittle muscles screamed their pain. After being motionless in a coma for almost two months, my tissue was twisted and frozen in strange directions. Julie's job was to somehow make me limber again through twice-daily exercises. My workouts to start were about a half an hour, then it took me about three hours of sleep to recover. My new routine became a half hour of stretching, followed by twice that much sleep. At the least.

Shortly after I arrived, late in the evening after visiting hours, nurse's aides lifted me onto a gurney and whisked me down a long hallway for pelvic x-rays. They left me in the hallway . . . and forgot about me. I waited in the barren, cold, dark corridor for a few hours—silently. I could not call for help; my throat hadn't healed from the tracheotomy. I couldn't roll over, much less sit up or walk. A two-month-old baby had more mobility. Had God forgotten me?

Eventually, a male nurse found me freezing in the hallway. He wheeled me in for x-rays, placed me on the table, reached under my hips to position me for the x-ray . . . and there it was. The most beautiful tattoo of a large Celtic cross adorned the inside of his buff right triceps. Love once again filled me. God had not forgotten me after all! I now knew He would continue to appear in the slightest ways, especially when I needed to be reminded of His presence—and the eternal place I had visited.

Every time the nurse and others adjusted me into different x-ray angles, sharp shooting pain seized and jolted my pelvis. I focused intently on his cross. The man noticed my eyes, and moved the cross closer. "You like it, don't you?" he asked. He gently guided my hand across its surface. We caught each other's eyes and both smiled haphazardly. I felt as innocent and limited as a three-year-old. He understood, and talked to me like I was his pretty little friend. After that event, he and the others made sure that when I arrived for x-rays, I was covered in a warmed blanket. They always wheeled me into the x-ray technician's area, even if someone else was already in there. My Celtic cross-tattooed nurse wasn't about to let anyone leave his little friend out in the cold again.

There was never a dull moment in the ward. What a House of Cards. By "cards," I mean the various patients. They were *characters*.

The ward floor was quite a trip. It was full of bizarre adventures and people. Or "cases," as the psychologists referred to us. Life was interesting and daunting. My first roomie was only there for a day or two before they moved her to another room; I was too deeply steeped in morphine and the goofy hazy feeling that accompanies a good drip to remember anything about him.

Fortunately, I had fantastic medical coverage, due to my husband's job as a radio sports announcer for the San Diego Chargers and the San Diego State Aztecs football teams. The coverage totaled one million dollars. I would use every dime of it and more. Because of it, I was always given an uninsured roommate. What did I care? My insurance was paying for the room; why not share half of it with someone less fortunate?

One morning, activity bustled on the other side of the curtain. A new roomie! I was so excited to have her, someone to talk with, someone I could encourage, and vice versa. Yippy!

However, it turned out quite differently. Grumbling and sharp shouting quaked from behind the curtain. The TV blared loudly and constantly through the night. The next morning, I could barely get up after feeling as if I had been in a battle zone all night. I completed very few of my stretches. Had I just taken a major step backwards?

Julie noticed. She wheeled me back to my room early to relax and try again later. No such luck. The TV droned as loudly as before. I called a nurse, who lowered the volume. Soon, I understood why it was so loud in the first place. Profanity of all kinds filled the air, flying from this woman's mouth. I buzzed the nurse again, and she gave me an explanation. My new roomie had some type of head trauma, and she was like a Tourette's soul trapped in an ugly hell. "I'll try not to notice," I told the nurse, hoping my inclination toward compassion would kick in, all the while thinking, "There for the grace of God go I." However, as much as I wanted to help both my roommate and the nurses, I couldn't take it. I lay awake all evening, crying and asking God to be with me, to protect me from evil.

The next day, I asked for her to be moved. "No," the nurse said firmly. "You have no say in who is in what room."

Later, my doctor entered the room while making his rounds. Even he could hardly focus with the TV and cursing filling the air. "I can't take it," I told him.

They moved her to the room across the hall.

Later, when I returned from my day at the therapy room, a new floor nurse and roommate greeted me. The nurse explained that the woman was an undocumented Hispanic with no insurance, had been in the hospital for nearly eight months, and received large numbers of family visitors on the weekends. "Will this be okay with you?" she asked. I looked over and saw a lovely, frail woman incapable of communicating. Except for her eyes. I knew how hard it was to be in that shell, unable to let anyone know how you felt.

We smiled at each other. I was happy to have her as a room-mate.

That weekend, her family showed up with little kids who soon became antsy. I had an idea. I turned to the many flowers, candies, and a new box of cookies I'd received, slid down my little skateboard-like, makeshift board to my wheelchair—but couldn't reach the cookies. Did I have enough strength to use my walker? I struggled across the room (about three feet, LOL) and reached down. I grabbed the cookies, but started losing my balance. I didn't want to fall, since my hips had been healing in a metal belt for the past two months. What if I broke my hips or punctured my lungs? Someone behind me suddenly caught me and boosted me upright. Hands held and guided me. I delivered the cookies to the other side of the curtain. "Comida," I said with a smile, using the only Spanish word I could think of. The little ones looked at their *abuela*, grandma, and smiled while taking only two cookies. "No, no," I said, handing over the entire box and closing the curtain.

I turned to see who had been holding me. *No one was there.* Once again, I realized, the hands of God were holding me lovingly, like they've held me up many times when I'm falling. This would repeat throughout my life for years to come.

A few doors down, a lively, handsome, rail thin, twenty-something man lived in a tented bed. I didn't know the circumstances of his accident, but he languished in the mental state of a five-year-old. His tented bed zipped closed, keeping him inside so he couldn't roam the halls. On occasion, they brought him out, and I was lucky enough to receive his visit in my room one day. We ate cookies and he smelled my flowers, sticking his nose deep inside them, just like a two-year-old. I wouldn't have been surprised to see pollen on the tip of his nose when he lifted up. He wiggled and giggled with delight while dancing around me, almost as though he was saying, *Look at me look at what I can do that you can't*! He existed in a place of sheer joy.

After our visit, the nurses zipped him back into bed. He wore his beloved basketball sweats, his Lakers hat firmly planted on his head with the brim up like a little kid, rather than a gangsta. A little basket hung inside the tent. He spent hours tossing and shooting a Nerf ball. During one of my later visits, I called play-by-play from my chair: "It's Magic, he's going in deep, he shoots, he scores! The crowd goes wild."

My husband's sports casting skills had rubbed off on me, despite my many attempts over the past fifteen years to limit my exposure to it—especially when it came to football. When you match a former collegiate and pro quarterback with a woman who never liked or understood why grown men pummel each other every Sunday afternoon, or the noxious locker room mentality that comes with it (*grunt, grunt, hike!*), well . . . let's just say we had other common interests, and I didn't quite fit in with the rest of the household on that one.

As it turned out, my little "call" of my friend's Nerf basketball prowess was magical for both of us, the only way we could interact effectively.

I attended two hours of therapy every day. We were now on our own; it was an honor system. Many of the patients would merely play and not work out. Not me: I wanted to walk, to again participate in the sports I loved. I wanted to play with my boys.

One day shortly after Thanksgiving, during therapy, a big buff football stud joined our ward. He was from Michigan, and had come to California to visit his uncle. It was his first trip to the Golden State. His uncle was about ten years older than him, and ten years younger than his mother, so he felt like his uncle was more like an older brother. This twenty-year-old had never taken a four-wheeling adventure, let alone seen the desert. He took his Thanksgiving break from college to partake in the excitement of off-road motocross at Gliamus, known as a haven to California desert rats. During his second ride, he flew over a sand dune. He lost control of the quad, flipping it and breaking his neck. Now he joined our gang of the feeble-yet-hopefuls, to learn how to live as a paraplegic. I have since thought to myself many times how Thanksgiving must have a new and perhaps not so thankful meaning to his mother or uncle. Julie said that the therapists hated Thanksgiving and Easter week, because their patient numbers always increased thereafter due to motorcycle and quad accidents.

This young man and I became friends and workout buddies. I had been a three-sport college athlete, and he had played football in both high school and college. He shared with me how he dreaded the coming conversation with his college coach, who had warned against his trip. I figured he had more worries than his coach's disappointment. Our focus and commitment to ourselves, and each other, was never to quit, to dig deep and give it our all, to put in as much as we could possibly endure and to handle as much pain as possible. Some of the other players joked that we were overachievers, teacher's pets. That would've been a first for me! The teacher's pet description, I mean . . . I am the overachieving type. Not so much in my high school years, when my boyfriend, the beach, my friends, and a lively mid-1970s party scene called out to me much more forcefully than my teachers, aside from one nasty little Marine woman (she was a high-ranking officer in the U.S. Marine Corps Reserve): "Brookhart! Are you Timothy Brookhart's little sister?"

"Yes."

"Then you sit right there."

She pointed to the desk nearest the door, figuring she would send me packing any time. I guess my brother got the best of her one too many times.

I'm a competitor. I don't like being outdone, even by my brother. Eventually, I said something in defense of a friend who told the teacher in no uncertain terms what to do. The teacher pointed her sharp little finger at me, and then at the door. I surely was no angel myself. I took two of my long strides, which filled her screen because of the micro shorts I was wearing, and I bailed. Not that it bothered me: I always did like sitting outside on a warm, sunny day.

However, in this ward I held an entirely different sentiment toward my paralyzed new friend. As far as I was concerned, he could outdo me; I was happy when he did. I said to him with a huge smile, "You only get out of life what you put into it." We'd chuckle and say "roll on."

I knew I was going to walk again. I had the luxury of having seen it during my life review in Heaven. Or should I say, my preview of what would come next. Unfortunately for this guy, he would never walk again—but he was determined to be a competitor and a life champion from his wheelchair.

Life in the Ward

My recovery became a case of painful, physical, and emotionally taxing drudgery. No one had told me the severity of my accident, yet several times each day in rehab, my psychologist reiterated that I had suffered some sort of brain damage. *Great.* What a little positive reinforcement can do. *Not!*

At first it was hard for me to retain information (sometimes, it still is), but I progressed in that area quickly at the Sharp Rehabilitation Center. My psychologist gave me reviews of basic questions and answers each day. She'd ask me the days of the week, the months and seasons, and then we moved on to numbers. She started off by giving me two numbers, which I repeated back to her. She moved on to three, four, or five numbers in a row. On the second or third day, she wanted me to give her the numbers backward from the order she had presented them. When I got to the point where I had to do this with seven-number sequences, I was not even close to saying them in reverse order. She flashed a cruel little smile, and then shot me down by loudly telling me I had head trauma. "This is something you will simply have to learn to accept," she said, her tone either mocking or condescending. I couldn't tell which.

This numbers test went on for another day. As before, I would do fine until we once again got to seven-number sequences. She kept making comments about my brain damage and memory, enough to rattle me to the point that I could barely recite them in the direct order, much less give them backwards. Again, she baited me, with what I consider negative reinforcement; her constant remark was, "You have brain damage." Nice.

I knew she thought her comments helped to motivate me. I finally asked her, "What is the significance of the number seven?" She said there are seven digits in phone numbers. I quickly informed her, "I never remembered phone numbers, even before my supposed brain damage. That's what paper and pencil are for. I keep my friends' numbers in my address book" (remember, this was before smart phones). I went on, full of myself. "In fact, phone numbers are actually ten numbers. Three are the area code, three the prefix, and the final four numbers are really all you need to remember, if you know the first two sets, then the final four is what narrows it down to a specific phone."

Ah hah! Gotcha with that one! I figured this argument out so quickly that I most certainly did not have the brain damage she kept referring to. I told her, "I do not appreciate your negative reinforcement. I'd like it if you'd step down from my case, and allow me the dignity of a new psychologist, one that will be more in tune with me and my need of a more positive way of motivation."

The next day, I was greeted by my new psychologist. We decided to move past numbers and let her assess my mental capacity.

Prior to my accident, I worked part time at Bates Nut Farm, giving educational talks about the history of the farm, nuts, bees, and pumpkins, and how they are all related to autumn and the Harvest Festival. Little did I know that these talks would become a practicing point to help test and improve my memory.

I worked each day with my new psychologist, focusing despite the buzzing from the high levels of morphine in my system. She asked me to practice the script I had once delivered to the school kids visiting Bates. Finally, some fun! While I related the memories of the kids and the farm, the psychologist actually gathered information about nature and farming from me. I shared stories about making scarecrows for the farm, festively trimming the farm trees, and dressing the shops for the holidays. I did all of this from my feeble, weakened state in my hospital bed, with no makeup, and a head of dirty unwashed hair. I also wore cheap men sweat pants with elastic waistbands, so I could have the dignity of dressing myself, as opposed to being embarrassed in one of those hospital robes, backside peeking open and all. God, how I missed a good zipper! I also missed being able to take my own shower, to brush my teeth at an actual sink, and to zip up a pair of pants or button a button. I felt humiliated by my inability to perform simple daily tasks; this seemed to include every aspect of daily life. Funny, the normal inanimate objects you miss when they are taken away.

I also participated in occupational therapy. I had many different coaches, as I liked to call them. My main physical therapist and number one coach, Julie, worked with my stretching and walking. My psychologist, coach two, focused on the mental part of learning to accept my new life challenges, and to understand what my new emotional and mental capabilities would become. The strength therapist, coach number three, worked on arm and leg flexibility. Then there was my occupational therapist with the honorary position, Debbie Domestic Coach Number Four, for daily life functions. I wish I could remember all their names, but his most of all. I asked each day, and, well . . . let's call him Peter. He was so wonderful, a sweet natured guy, thirty-ish, slim with dark hair and a great sparkling smile.

Peter had to teach me basic domestic duties from my wheelchair. This crushed me. I mean, after all, this was my life, my job—my worth was as a mom and a wife for the past fifteen years. Do you know how odd it is to load a dishwasher from a wheelchair? It was so ridiculous, funny, and yet depressing, I almost wet my pants every day laughing at myself.

The bottom of the barrel came when he taught me how to cook. He gave me a box of a brownie mix, an egg, a wooden spoon, and a measuring cup. He cut the box open by slicing a *T* down the center of the box and folding open the sides like a book. He instructed me on breaking an egg, gave me a measuring cup to fill with water, and then pour into the box and stir with the wooden spoon. Talk about your workout! If he hadn't walked me through each step, including how to turn on the oven, that cake still wouldn't be baked. After quite the exertion of energy to perform this task, I was afraid of how much more it would take to fill the cake pan. But I needn't have worried. "You cook the cake in the box," Peter said. Humiliation complete—or so I thought.

I took part in my group workout with coach number one, Julie. It was supposed to be fun. We played wheelchair volleyball, using a balloon in place of a regulation volleyball. This hurt me the most inside, because I had played on my college volleyball team. One day, we split into teams, in our wheelchairs, four on each side of the droopy, four- to five-foot-high net. We rolled around the makeshift court, banging that large purple balloon over the net toward an opponent and using our teamwork to not bump into each other. Balloons don't flow quite as precisely as an actual volleyball.

I became so distracted by my own weaknesses and inabilities that it was hard to even follow the game. I looked to the side of the room and saw a face I thought I knew. The man sat quietly, smiling at me. *I know that guy; I know that I know him, what is his name?*

My memory did not help me. *Damn . . . this is something I'm going to have to deal with for a long time, and it might just drive me crazy.*

I wheeled over to him. He stood and hugged me, tears sparkling in his eyes. "Martha, I'm so glad God blessed you and you're still here with us. Wow . . . how we prayed for you." After talking, he tried to cheer up the conversation with, "You are looking great. I've been watching you move; I didn't want to interrupt the game."

I was so grateful for his words, spoken as if I were in a real volleyball game and still possessed my athletic abilities. I completely loved this guy for his words, but for the life of me, I could not access his name from my memory bank.

Embarrassed, I finally asked. "Don't be embarrassed," he said. "You haven't seen me for nearly eight years, since Aaron's sixth birthday when all us guys went flying. I'm Bobby Melina."

Duhhhh, my brain screamed at me. Of course! Bobby!

What made Bobby drive out of his way to visit me at the hospital on the very day at the exact moment I needed a lift? How did Bobby know I needed to hear a compliment, one that gave me the belief that I was still an athlete? He needed it, too. He and his wife, Cindy, had prayed fiercely; I guess he needed the validation that God had heard his prays. Why didn't he send a card instead? We hadn't seen each other in eight years.

I think it was providence, not coincidence.

Since that day, I believe we need to listen to those intuitions. When we feel we should do something for someone, then we should. No questions asked, and no expectations. The pleasures in a person's life can come in the smallest compliments. You never know what another person needs to hear, or how a simple positive comment can make all the difference to them, their day, or their life. When I get those thoughts today, I try to always pay the compliment. I try to say and do the right thing for the other person without concern for what I might need. I certainly haven't mastered it—I suck at it some days—but I keep trying. I know I'm not very forgiving of what people do, and often I can't believe what people will say . . . or what will come out of my own mouth, for that matter. God, the Divine power, showed me that love is the most important thing we possess, and we need to show, express, and give it, and I plan on doing just that.

After a week or two in rehab, my dear friend Kris Reilly came to visit. We had shared many adventures while raising our boys together in their many sports. I was a bit nervous about what I wanted to tell her, because I had encountered a few trials with some of my Church lady friends. For starters, they wondered "why" I was a good friend with a Mormon bishop's wife. To me, one religion or the other does not make the person. Instead, the key elements of a friend are their lifestyles, actions, and most importantly, how they treat others. These things matter to me; the people who possess them are my core friends. So here was one of my most beloved friends.

Here goes . . . I told Kris I had been with an Angel. She believed me! She didn't cut me off, get up tight, or think I was crazy. Now I had someone with whom I could share my secret, without judgment. What a comfort—I'd thought I was losing my mind! Every night, when I fell asleep, my mind would fill with visions of Heaven, but during the days, I felt like I was trapped inside a ward of misfits and broken souls. Kris's visit really helped me out.

I kept thinking of us, the *wardies,* as residents of the island of misfit toys, to borrow from the holiday TV classic *Rudolph the Red-Nosed Reindeer.* My mind kept taking me back to this Christmas special from my childhood. Happy as we all may have been in the ward, we were the outcast toys of the iceberg island with the abominable snowman. I was the dentist with the perpetual smile. I was constantly trying to find the positive, and most importantly, my way out of the center.

Finding my way out . . . hum, now at least I had told Kris and she was a believer. She shared with me how bad my accident had been, that everyone was shocked I had made it, that I had been pronounced dead, a CRAMS Zero, and then in a coma for two months. Now I was smiling and laughing with her, telling her about Angels.

The Christmas season and its angels had come to the ward. We were wheeled into the main lobby room, where we saw a barren, not so top-of-the-line fake Christmas tree. Our task was to decorate this sad specimen of a Christmas tree from our wheelchairs. The aides brought out cardboard boxes trickled with the most dreadful and tattered ornaments. We were handed one tacky ornament at a time, with no rhyme or reason as to who was handed which ornament. This drove me crazy. I had decorated my own trees, other people's houses, and Bates Nut Farm for years. To my way of thinking, the placement and color scheme is always done with a mathematical and artistic precision. Not even my little boys' tree was random.

This tree was different. Our sad little ward group sang Christmas carols, drank lukewarm hot chocolate (they didn't want anyone burning their lips or hot liquid dribbling down their chins), and we diligently hung the few sparkling stars. Despite our circumstances, I believe we all felt great joy in our hearts.

Finally, we finished the tree. It was full of ugly little sparkles that covered the tree, but, it sparkled only three feet and below. Tee hee, smiles in place, we looked at it while knowing you can only stretch so high while seated.

A special visitor saw me for a few days in rehab. Julie had arranged a specialist, whose name I cannot remember. This lady, a true angel, had been in the Vietnam War, where she helped wounded pilots learn to walk again. She learned that if you watch the way a baby learns to walk, perhaps it would make sense for an adult to start this way as well. Hmmm, why couldn't the trained doctors see it as simply? She would teach me that I must first learn to crawl before I learn the balance of walking. This was exactly why Nancy was here. Well, I'll call her Nancy for this.

Nancy put me on the torturer bench, as I liked to call it. I got on my knees on the slick vinyl surface. I had to roll over at least three turns . . . excruciating! I had to do this all by myself, unassisted by Julie.

Next, I had to push myself up to a dog stance, on my hands and knees. Sounds simple and should be, right? Oh my God, what a toughie! After I got up I had to rock back and forth, just like a baby. My mind was full of *head forward, butt back, forward, back, forward.* Playing a game with myself, I imagined I could hear a va . . . room, va . . . room . . . and I was the race car on the starting line. I'd rock for a few minutes, then move on to the almost impossible, moving my right knee forward, picking up my right arm, and extending my hand.

After falling on my face several times, Julie explained that I needed to focus. I was working on training my right brain to have control over my body. Nancy was telling me to move my right knee and then my left arm, but my body kept doing it right, right, right. I thought back to the cadets at the school my dad served as dean, the Army-Navy Academy. *Left, left . . . left, right, left!* I worked that cadence into my exercises and within three days I had it down. Now whenever I hear baby steps, I laugh to myself and think *right, right . . . right, left, right.*

Years later, I saw Nancy on a special TV documentary concerning how she taught many pilots to walk through crawling first.

I remember the day I watched it. I saw her, stunned, and watched her put the wounded warriors through the exercise. The memories flooded back, and I began to cry uncontrollably.

I was improving. I was able to take a few steps on the even bars, and I didn't fall once! Julie had worked hard to loosen the rigid tissue of my frozen shoulders, and we hoped that with continued therapy, I'd be relieved of this pain sometime soon. My mind was becoming less foggy by the day, and my memory was starting to show signs of returning. I was far more alert then I had been in a very long time.

Meanwhile, my husband did a great thing to motivate me. He blew up photos of my family and boys to poster size and hung them next to my bed. Whenever friends asked what they could send me, he suggested individually wrapped candy or cookies, which would serve as my bribes. They served as motivators for the nurses, too. Every time a nurse came into my room, I'd offer them a piece of candy. When they'd say, "Oh no, thank you, I'm too busy right now," I'd say, "Take one—put it in your pocket to snack on later—take two." These little chocolates went a long way. Whenever they came back—and believe me, they did!—they would get a chocolate and look at my pictures.

This method worked. The nurses that stopped in couldn't help but ask *who everyone was*. I'd look at the photos and think it over. This simple step made me speak out loud and focus on my reason for fighting (my boys). It bolstered my intent to improve. I strained to remember everyone's name in the pictures. It's funny in a way to try and remember your siblings' first names after a mere forty years of knowing them. Now, it was a hard thing to do.

The time was nearing for my final test. Julie told me I had to meet with the hospital ward staff and plead my case to be released. I would have to walk with my walker outside, cross the street, and take a step off the curb. *Help! The Curb!*

On that morning, I had to go in alone; my husband could not attend. His no-show made me livid. I was rattled and excited, but also scared to death of what they'd choose for me. Eight people sat around a long conference table: Julie, myself, the head nurse, the chief doctor (whom I had only met once), Peter (my occupational therapist), the psychologist (the negative motivator I'd asked to step down), my strength trainer, and a speech therapist with whom I'd only worked a few times. Each gave their evaluation of my progress. I listened as they spoke about me in third person, as if I were not there. I kept hearing I would be released to go home soon, which really excited me. They all spoke highly of me . . . until we arrived at the psychologist, who started by saying I denied the existence of my brain trauma. I listened for a while . . .

Finally, I had enough. I needed to protect myself and the possibility of my release. I don't know how prisoners feel when they appear before the parole board, but this had to be similar. I was confined to a place against my will, and I wanted out. I needed this panel to see my side, so I shared the story of the numbers exercise and recited some phone numbers. The Chief Doctor smiled broadly, reached for my form and signed it. He told Julie all I needed was to take my walk. Then he looked at the Psychologist, his eyes suddenly hard, and told her that a positive attitude was always the best motivation.

I hadn't been outside in almost three months. The December sunlight seemed intense, sharp and bright, but my real fear was the CURB. It was only seven inches high, but it looks more like seventy. They wanted me to step off this cliff? Yes they did, with my walker; what could be so difficult about it? To me, those seven inches felt like a high dive, as if I had been asked to jump off a thirty-foot cliff. I did jump off a thirty-foot cliff years later in India, and I'm here to tell you that I felt far more fear and trepidation over this curb.

Finally, I stepped off, stumbling a bit. I did it! Not so fast . . . Julie then made me repeat the simple step two more times. That left me exhausted, but it meant I could receive my release and go home to my babies, my joy.

It was time for my new life to begin.

Life in the Fast Lane—
Going Home—
Steps to a New Life

Freedom! Release! After three and a half weeks in rehab prison, I'm a free girl!

I packed my bags . . . or should I say, my one brown paper bag. I loaded it up with one extra pair of sweat pants, three tee shirts, many get well cards, and my enlarged family photos. I was so ready to go home to my babies Aaron and Nate, my husband, my dogs Stormy and Bo, and my friends.

Most of all, I was ready to get back to my life. *Game on! I'm prepared for the many months in my wheelchair, and the continued months of rehabilitation. I can't wait to get home . . . but I'm petrified of what lies ahead.*

Meanwhile, San Diego radio and TV icon Ted Leitner knew of my upcoming release. Ted is a San Diego broadcasting institution, the radio voice of the San Diego Chargers and Padres for more than thirty years. He is a very warm, gregarious, down to earth man, with a giving heart to match. Ted understood that I was deeply frightened of riding in a car. I wasn't sure what type of reaction I would have. All I wanted was a pillow and blanket to hide my head while on the road. What did Ted do? He arranged for me to make the seventy-five-minute ride home in a limo. As he put it, "Take her any place she wants to go."

Well, you don't have to tell me twice.

First things first. I was so sick and tired of hospital food, and I craved something with some spice . . . *some good old California Mexican food.* However, I was afraid of the shock the spices might put my body through. We asked the driver what he would recommend as a quick meal with spices. The young driver instantly knew of a Chinese place nearby, and we headed off. The driver was on autopilot, not thinking about where and how he was driving. Fittingly, he turned into the drive-through. Have you ever seen a limo go down a drive through? It's not all that easy, with twenty feet of car trailing behind. A few failed attempts later, I uncorked a hearty and deeply needed belly laugh.

The driver walked inside to place the order. I had no idea what I wanted to eat, but we knew it couldn't be too spicy, or it might completely mess up the ride home, not to mention my still frail state. The meal's scent entered the vehicle before the bag, which I opened. The smell of the first white carton filled my nostrils. It was pure sweetness, with a tang of vinegar. Yum! I wanted those wontons and egg rolls, but first I enjoyed just looking at them. It had been a long time since any food I took intravenously or ate had color to it, much less a distinct aroma. One crunch, and the mouthful of sweet and sour sauce ran across my taste buds, making my mouth water. As I swallowed it was hard to keep myself from drowning in my own saliva, I was completely content! Even though the crispy crust scratched down the sides of my throat as I swallowed, this didn't bother me. I figured this was something I'd be willing to live with, forever, if it meant my mouth would water like this again. I was in complete ecstasy.

We drove north up Interstate 15 from San Diego. My fear of being in a car again had ruined my sleep for the past few days. I was certain it would be a nerve racking ride between the speeds, the jam-packed lanes, and the weaving of a road I feared would be filled with holiday travelers, their minds everywhere but straight ahead. I looked out the thankfully tinted window; the reflective glint from the other cars hurt my eyes. I had been inside darkened rooms for the past two months, so the sunshine made my eyes water and blink.

I held on tight to my hubby's hand—in between bites of egg roll, of course. I wanted to see him, to share my happiness with him. It was different than before, and I felt closer to him. I sort of chanted to myself, "It's okay, girl, you've come a long way, baby, God loves you," while almost screaming, much more furtively, "Okay, Angel, where are you now . . . help!"

I wanted to not let my mind go topsy-turvy with the fear reeling inside my body, a fear that was causing my palms to soak in sweat. I kept waiting for the limo to flip heel to toe, but thankfully, we just rolled along smoothly.

We asked the limo driver to stop at the trauma unit of Palomar Hospital, so we could thank the medical staff for their fantastic and loving treatment. It was due to the God-given talents of Dr. David Cloyd, the talented trauma unit, and all the nursing staff that I survived the accident. These nurses were angels on Earth; they had been by my side and helped me when I needed them the most.

As we pulled up, I felt myself being pulled back to that terrible night. When I had arrived at the trauma unit, I was classified as a CRAMS Zero—the lowest prospect for survival. On a battlefield or major accident scene, the first responders would have black-tagged me when triaging the victims. Likewise, most trauma units would have given up, but not Palomar Hospital. I thank God daily that they didn't give up on me.

I was wheeled into the emergency room. After it was explained how I had been saved in the trauma unit nearly three months earlier, they ushered us into the unit. Soon, a few nurses walked out. When they saw me, they couldn't believe their eyes. One flashed the biggest smile, went back through the door, and brought out more nurses. I noticed a walker positioned in the hallway, and motioned with my eyes for the walker to be brought to me. My husband knew exactly what I wanted. We had a way of doing this, of understanding what the other person wanted or meant by our movements, one of the benefits of being married for fifteen years.

Without a word, he placed the walker in front of my chair. When I tried to stand, the nurses' already-surprised faces opened up in shock. I stood there wobbling, but standing, then I spoke raspily while smiling at a male nurse in his mid-fifties. He had been on duty the night of my accident. Tears filled his eyes, confirming just how bad off they had thought I was. "God bless you," he said in a choked-up, fatherly voice.

I smiled. "He already has," I said. Little did I know that this would become one of my favorite sayings.

As I stood and choppily talked with the nurses, they informed me I resided on their Wall of Fame. "Why?" I asked.

Their answer made sense: I had been classified as a CRAMS Zero, their one and only, and now lived to tell about it. It was unheard of. A CRAMS test measures circulation, respiration, abdominal condition, motor skills, and speech for incoming emergency room patients. It is equivalent to an Apgar test they give newborn babies; it measures how the circulatory system and brain are functioning, the two systems that sustain life. Someone later told me Palomar once admitted a woman who ranked CRAMS Three. She survived, but in a vegetative state. Now they welcomed back a CRAMS Zero, their very own. After I transferred down to Scripps for rehabilitation, none of them knew what my outcome would be. They could only hope and pray. They all knew I shouldn't even be alive.

Yet here I was, standing and talking. You can't get rid of me that easily! The visit uplifted all of us. They had accepted me into their family of special patients.

I was then ushered to the Intensive Care Unit, where my family and I had spent too many days and nights to count. While being wheeled down the hall, I heard the voice I will always remember: the soft Persian accent. Following my life-saving eight-hour surgery, before I fell into my medically induced coma, this Persian voice said, "You are so beautiful; you are lucky your fine face isn't hurt." The nurse who possessed the heavenly voice scrubbed my face free of road grit and the fine pieces of glass sprayed over it.

I remembered her voice distinctly. After she said this, I thought, *Thank God,* because it felt as if my face had been ripped off. My head didn't do so well, either. When my boys came in to say their good-byes after the accident, they didn't really recognize me, because my head was swollen nearly to the size of a pumpkin.

Now I wanted to stop her to thank her, but she was already gone. We stopped at the ICU nurses' desk, and I thanked them for giving so much love to my family. I described the nurse with the perfect voice, and they told me her name. They said they would tell her my story and how her comment helped me. I wasn't mentally able to remember her name, though I'm sure it's as lovely as the sound of her voice. I'm sure she will never know how much her simple comments helped me rest easier during those two months in the coma.

I arrived home to so much joy. The security guards at the front gate of our neighborhood walked out of their shed, and reached inside the limo with smiles and hugs. They told me how much they had missed me, and that they were available if I needed anything at all.

I was one of the few younger folks that lived in the Pauma Valley community. I had a habit of playing Chinese Fire Drill with my boys when we drove home from school. We'd stop at the gate, and I'd tell them, "Now go!" Aaron, Nate, Miles, and any other friends would jump out of the car, run circles around it, and land in a different seat. The guards loved it because we brought some youthful frivolity to their otherwise dull days.

The limo cruised past the fourth and fifth fairway of the golf course. The bright sunlight on the course highlighted the lovely crisp freshly manicured greenery. It felt so good to be able to watch the golfers walking the greens. I thought to myself, *This is going to be my daily motivation; I'll watch my neighbors golf until I'm green with envy.* I didn't think "green with envy" would become a reality for me, but it did.

The limo rolled into our driveway. The large front doors swung open, and Aaron and Nate ran out. I desperately tried to get that seat belt unhooked, but then I noticed for the first time that I couldn't work my fingers smoothly. I had none of my agility or strength. Pain flamed through my knuckles as I fumbled with the belt. I didn't care. I would endure any pain of any level right now. I wanted out. I wanted to hug my babies. I looked at them. *Oh man, they look older!* They had undergone too much.

It was December 20, and I was home. There couldn't be a better Christmas gift ever. I looked around my beautiful home; to my joy, it was radiant, completely covered in full holiday season decor. "Do you remember when Kris called you at the hospital and asked where you stored your Christmas decorations?" my husband asked.

"Yes."

"Well, Kris Reilly and Margaret Redden came by right after Thanksgiving to decorate. They said you would have wanted things to seem normal for the boys, and they figured this is exactly what you would have done for them."

Kris and Margaret knew how much I loved decorating for Christmas, something I did for work, family, friends, and joy. There is nothing in my world greater than friends who completely understand all of your individual tastes . . . and quirks, for that matter. My girlie friends' generosity completely overwhelmed me. They wanted Aaron and Nathan to be surrounded with love for Christmas, and delivered our holiday cheer. The rest of the community turned out as well.

Carolers of several different churches arrived nightly. We listened to their beautiful songs and shared the multitude of cookies and sweets that other friends had dropped off earlier in the day. The refrigerator was constantly full of food from friends. It seemed that every church in the town included me on their prayer list, and now they knew I was home. They were all so thankful. I was the spark during Christmas that confirmed their faith, and how truly God had answered their prayers.

My second night home, around 6:30 p.m., carolers from the Episcopal Church down the street converged at the door. My mother-in-law had already put me to bed; she and I had not enjoyed much warmth in our relationship, but on this night, she helped me slide into the bed, pulled the heavy covers up to my chin, bent over while patting my hand, and kissed my forehead lightly. We smiled into each other's eyes. It was a special moment.

Then I found out there were visitors. *Get me up!* I longed to see their faces, but I didn't have the strength to get up. Nathan opened my bedroom door so I could listen to it all. He smiled. "Isn't it nice, Mommy? It's Christmas, and this is the true meaning of what Christmas is all about." So much knowledge filled his eleven-year-old soul. He was overjoyed.

I motioned for him to come close. "Nate, be sure to give them some of the cookies," I whispered.

He loved this moment; it meant he and his brother could finally taste the sweets!

The community outpouring continued throughout the week. Carolers and visitors arrived from the Mormon Church, the Catholic Church, Pauma Valley Community Church, Ridgeview Church, and Valley Center Community Church. All my boys and I would listen to the carolers' beautiful songs, but now I was so enveloped by the wonderful lyrics that each song seemed new. You can only imagine how much more meaning they carried.

My dogs, Stormy and Bo, earned many brownie points because they became very protective of me. They started sitting in front of me so no one could get close. Bo even liked to snarl and growl, showing as much fang as possible. I found it funny because before the accident, I barely acknowledged him, with most of my love being trained on Stormy. The boys had wanted Bo, so he was part of us, but now Bo was truly one of my boys. Later in his life, when he was sick, I let him sleep on my bed. This was not something I would have allowed, but he'd melted my heart with his loving protection. Yes, I had changed.

I wanted desperately for this Christmas to be just as perfect as all our other Christmases. In the past, I worked at Bates Nut Farm during the holidays, simply to have the freedom to lavish my boys with the feeling (if not the objects) that they had it all, that their lives were special. I saved for ski trips to Utah, the coolest clothes for school, and Christmas toys of all kinds. But this year was different. I had been too busy healing in a coma to go shopping!

I was freaking out. I couldn't walk or drive. I wasn't really sure how to answer a phone, much less dial it, so that left dial-and-drop shopping out of the picture.

What to do for the boys? What could I give them for Christmas gifts? I had no idea, but I focused, visualized, believed that somehow, something would happen . . .

Time was running out. On Christmas Eve, we attended the service at Pauma Valley Community Church. Their youth group had been very good to Nathan during this ordeal, and my mother in-law enjoyed meeting with the ladies group. The singing was music to my ears. Normally, I didn't like singing in church. Let's just say my singing voice would never be compared to Paula Abdul, Jewel, Sara MacLachlan or Carrie Underwood (ask my sister; it's hereditary). Plus, I never knew the more modern songs they sang. We drove home with our hearts and souls filled. I was exhausted, but yet, what to offer as my gift to the boys . . .

Suddenly, out of deepest space, it came to me, a moment of enlightenment, and a feeling deep inside. *The gift.*

I called the boys into the hallway. I was home for only four days, but I wanted to give them back their strong, normal mom, no matter what it took. I needed to prove to them I would give everything within myself towards this recovery effort. I remembered visions I was shown in Heaven, specifically, what would happen to Aaron and Nathan if I remained on the other side. What I saw instantly gave me the conviction to come back. They needed me, and I still needed them.

I placed my walker in front of my wheelchair, firmly gripped the handles, and pulled myself up. While teetering awkwardly and gritting my teeth, I pushed the walker away and shoved it rolling about three feet down the hall.

I smiled at the boys. "Merry Christmas! I love you both very much, I'm going to show you mommy is back, and I'll do whatever it takes to be me again."

With one hand flattened firmly against each wall, I took one step. Then another. And another. I willed my dull stumps of driftwood, my limbs, to carry my new, lightweight frame down the hall. I managed three more steps before I plopped into my wheelchair, exhausted. My heart and face erupted into full smiles. I did it. I pulled it off!

The boys cheered. It sounded like a full auditorium hooting and hollering. Tears filled their eyes as huge smiles crossed their faces. "Mommy will walk again," I said.

Christmas gift? Delivered! God's Christmas blessing? Intact! "Yes, you can," my Angel whispered deep inside my being.

She was right. She had not left me alone after our time in Heaven.

Never again would I need to explain the true meaning of Christmas to Aaron and Nathan. Love visited and filled us from every direction. What a Christmas!

Afterward, the time had come to begin the truly difficult work.

Chapter 10

Determination and Belief

Just a week after my amazing Christmas, on New Year's Day 2000, I sat at home, alone, and growing sick of my weakened state. I realized in a wheelchair I would be left out often. Not a great state of mind with which to bring in the new millennium. Nonetheless, my determination to compete again in life, or anything at all, roared within me. I called the wheelchair rental company and left a message: "Pick up the wheelchair tomorrow. I will not be needing it any longer."

This decision upset my husband. I can still hear him admonishing me. "What are you thinking? You need that chair." He may not have meant them as a negative, but I hated those words. With that, my family remembered something about me: my determination. We created a new game with each other, competing to see who would tell the other "I love you" first. That night, we put tennis balls on the front legs of my walker and then adjusted my cane to the right height. Time to show my determination! I was going to give it my all; you can't do that while rolling around in a wheelchair, unless you're paralyzed. Which I wasn't.

A few days later, I wrote a New Year's letter to my friends. I titled it, "My Thank You Gift is a Gift from God—an Angel."

This letter marked the first time I wrote about any part of the accident. It took me nearly three days to write, since I had lost virtually all of the small motor skills in my hands. I had used a computer at work, and played games with the boys at home like "You Don't Know Jack," and helped them research information for homework projects. I also stored simple household information on our home computer.

When I peered at the machine now, it looked unfamiliar, I knew I was supposed to know how to use it, but I had no idea how to even turn it on. It seemed that with every life task, I needed to ask for some kind of assistance. This was a true challenge for me. I had been the one offering help throughout my kids' lives, and taking care of myself before then. Now, I needed to be on the receiving end.

The help I received overwhelmed me, in a good way. Friends and acquaintances practically fought over the task of driving me to physical therapy three times a week. The fact that I was more accustomed to giving than receiving made it hard, but I smiled as best I could through the mental fog in which my brain was saturated. I couldn't undertake, participate in, or even comprehend the planning, so my girlfriends Colleen Heublein, Chris Wilkerson, and Kris Reilly got to work and split up lists of friends, each taking a different group (I was a joiner, so I had several groups). This terrific trio organized meals each night, and countless rides to therapy. These rides gave me a time each day when I could try to converse with another adult. This was a form of therapy in itself, this daunting job of learning how to form and deliver complete sentences on the fly. It was also such a pleasurable break from my isolation of home.

Once I finished physical therapy, I longed for companionship. My husband was always gone it seemed, whether to work, playing golf, or hanging out with his friends. When he was home, we didn't talk that much. He couldn't stand hearing me stutter, nor how I spoke in chopped-up sentences. I needed to ask directions again and again, even on the simplistic things on the computer. When I stuttered, he became a ten-year-old boy and would repeat back to me my stuttered sentence, trying to show me what I sounded like, which only made me more self-conscious and cause my stuttering to get worse. I believed he loved his tall, statuesque, athletic wife, not the person before him whose leg dragged behind a walker and who couldn't even pick up a gallon of milk to fill her sons' cereal bowls. That tennis-playing, fast-running, strong-swimming, big-wave bodysurfing version of me was gone. The accident had rendered her a memory that became more distant with each passing day.

Physical therapy was both my salvation and curse. I rode off with my friends to the office of David Nashida, my new friend and physical therapist at North County Physical Therapy. That was the salvation. Quickly, I formed a love-hate relationship with physical therapy; I loved David but hated the pain. We started with stretching and ultrasound to warm the muscles, and moved on to standing wall bends or the stationary bike, in order to strengthen my legs and hips. I also needed to strengthen my core muscles, which had been sliced down the middle during surgery. Stronger core muscles would give me the ability to walk with more stability.

After a few weeks, David promoted me to pool exercises. I had been swimming since I was two or three. I remember my mom teaching me by taking me in the ocean to her waist and dropping me. As I scratched toward her, she kept backing up, while showing me what stroke to take with my arms. I was the youngest of five kids and we spent each day of the summer at the beach, or at Army-Navy Academy's Olympic sized pool. If she was going to have any freedom, she needed me to learn—fast. I had been a water baby from that point on. When summer hit in San Diego, all we needed was to just add water, and we were set.

Now I watched people being lowered into the water. I felt the pool's 80-degree temperature, and knew I wanted to submerge myself. *Would I be okay?* My biggest worry was modesty. I worried how was I going to dress myself in my bathing suit, an independent chore. I arrived the next day in my suit and baggy workout pants, ready. I did my entire land workout, and then asked David, "Now do I get to go in the pool?"

He hadn't planned on me moving to the pool for another week or so, but I flashed him my biggest smile, and, well, my not-so-finest bathing suit. What's a therapist to do? Like a true coach, he put me in the game. While the warm water made me feel whole,

I struggled. Believe me: I was no powerful swimmer anymore. I stood and held on desperately to the side. Then I started floating and giggling like an eighteen-month-old baby. Before long, I quickly moved on to water aerobics.

David knew I lived on a golf course, and that it was an important factor in our lives. He used that to his advantage to motivate me. In the back room of his office, they had a state-of-the-art ceiling-high tracking and swing screen to smack away at golf balls. He promised me that once I could complete all the physical therapy exercises, he would move me up to practicing my golf swing. "You surely will be able to golf again," he added.

What a far-fetched idea! Who had the head injury? Me? Or him? Well, I figured, if he was willing to promise, I was willing to put my belief into him. *Four!*

My girlfriend Chris Wilkerson also took me to a Rolfer, a holistic system of soft tissue manipulation that organizes alignment and movement of various body areas. Rolfers move the fascia (connective tissue) until they believe it is operating in conjunction with the muscles in a more optimal relationship. In my case, the fascia of my muscles was all out of whack and placement.

That wasn't all. In addition to physical manipulation of tissue, Rolfing uses a combination of active and passive movement. Skeletal muscles often work in opposing pairs called the "agonist" and the "antagonist," one contracting, the other relaxing. The theory is that "bound up" fasciae often restrict opposing muscles from functioning in concert. The (painful) aim is to manually separate the fibers of bound-up fasciae to loosen them and allow effective movement. There is also an association between pent-up emotions and muscle tension. My body tissue would have memory from the accident, and boy did it!

We arrived at a condo to the smells of sage and incense. I was introduced to Blue, a unique sort of cosmic guy. I thought, *I'm going to expose my whole scarred body, inside and out, to him?* I hadn't been around anyone like him for a very long time, so his healthy organic lifestyle and high energy became a source of learning. Blue dug deeply (and painfully) into each muscle and worked on the flexibility of my body. He closed each session with chimes from Tibetan crystal bowls with which he circled my body. His purpose was to remove negative energy and to help heal my soul. This was a completely new concept to me, but I appreciated it and wanted to learn more.

I looked into other ways to heal more quickly. My friend Chris's husband, Wayne Wilkerson, was a prosthetic developer and international speaker at Scope Orthotics & Prosthetics, one of the leading sources of prosthetics in the world. He served as my unofficial walking coach. He knew his business; he makes prosthetic limbs for clients from around the world, even professional athletes. I figured if he could teach someone how to walk with a fake limb, then he should be able to teach me and my soggy driftwood leg how to walk. Our friendship was just another of God's wonderful placements in my life. We don't always know why we have certain friends, but then something happens, and the real reason of our life plan is placed directly in front of our eyes.

I faced one more major challenge: my growing dependence on morphine, my painkilling companion since the accident. My doctors wanted to drop me down a notch to Vicodin. I had watched an *Oprah* show on people addicted to prescription drugs, which made me realize that Vicodin is just as addictive. I feared replacing one possible addiction with another. That didn't make any sense to me.

I took matters into my own hands. Sometimes, I can get a little obsessed about things—as I did in this case. I set my plan. "Don't give me any morphine, no matter how badly I want it, and regardless of what nasty things I might say to you," I said to a family member I'd asked to see me through this.

For the next three days, I endured the hell of sweating it out cold turkey. I lay on our living room floor tiles, trying to stay cool, sweat covering my body. The lack of morphine after five months caused an excruciating withdrawal, the physical pain of which I had never felt before. I asked, pleaded, begged, screamed, ranted, and raved, *"Get me some morphine; I don't care how!"*

It was a different pain than what I suffered after my accident. This rose from my tissues. How my muscles screamed in agony!

One morning I even grabbed at my caretaker's ankles while lying on the tile floor in a thick sweat. "Give me something . . . anything!" I pleaded. The boys would be out of school for the summer soon and I didn't want to behave like this in front of my future men. It was kick it now or never.

Prior to this experience, I had always thought of drug addicts as lowlifes. I figured, *You made your bed, now lie in it.* I was taught that if you screwed up on something, you had to fix it yourself. My three days of withdrawal agony changed my view. Drug addiction really is a physical addiction (not to mention the emotional, mental, and spiritual agony), and withdrawals are truly excruciatingly painful.

You would think kindnesses were easily extended to me by passersby, well-wishers, and the like. That happened most of the time, but not always. I had a large scar from my tracheotomy, which caught on my larynx. Whenever I swallowed, it pulled upward, making an unsightly *V* in my throat. A not-so-kind woman pointed this out during a luncheon. "Why on earth don't you wear a scarf to cover that up?" she asked. Or something like that. It didn't matter—I felt like she'd just stabbed me.

Later, this same woman stood in the pro shop of Pauma Valley Country Club, complaining that I was a nuisance when I was learning to walk steps. Every day, I would walk up and down the steps in front of the golf shop. The pros told her I was welcome there, and how honored and happy they were that I was there for them to watch over. The steps were softened by slick, resistant padding, along with a railing that gave me the security I needed. Amazing! These pros were my cheerleaders, always encouraging me along the way. I knew the rest of my neighborhood was full of many people that did not fall into this woman's level of self-absorption. They were so kind and giving to me.

My friend, Jeff, is a perfect example. As I was recovering, he saw me limping around the streets and always supported me with his positive encouragement, confidence-building comments, and ready smile. I never forgot him. Apparently, he didn't forget me, either. Thirteen years later, in Spring 2013, I joined my sweetheart,

Bob, at his weekly running group in Oceanside . . . and there was Jeff! Now in his mid-sixties, he remains an avid runner and fitness buff. He gave me a big hug, and asked if I was joining the group. "I'm going to walk and jog a little," I said.

"Are you training for anything?" he asked.

"Yes . . . the Missoula (MT) Half Marathon in July."

His eyes lit up . . . . He could hardly believe what he heard. Early in the fall, I came to running group again, and told Jeff how I came in under three hours in the half marathon. He broke into a wall-to-wall smile, giving me a big hug. You can't break three hours in a 13.1-mile race without doing some running along the way, and Jeff knew it.

Flash forward to late January 2014, when Bob saw Jeff at the running group. As they ran a four-mile stretch along the beach together, Jeff asked, "Where's Martha? How is she? What's she been up to?"

"Well, she just ran-walked the Carlsbad Half Marathon with her sister the other day," Bob told him.

"That is the most amazing and determined woman I've ever met. She's a walking miracle," Jeff said. "Tell her we want her at group more often."

I already knew that life presented people willing to kick you down if you let them. I determined to find more Jeffs in the world, the positive people, along with the positive moments and outcomes every day.

As my recovery continued, I found myself opening up more, and more people seemed to take a genuine interest in my story. I got a call from Kris, asking if I would share with a few of the boys at her house. "Sure," I said. "Can you send them down?"

Soon, there was a knock at my door. There stood two young Mormon missionaries. While I am not Mormon, I definitely have a deep respect for the religion. I also have a pretty direct personal tie; I am directly descended from founder Joseph Smith. The boys came in, and we visited for about an hour. I didn't have anything to fix for lunch, but my fridge was still stocked with an overabundance of Christmas cookies. If you have ever spent time with Mormon missionaries, or Elders as they are called, you know they appreciate good meals or snacks!

We had a wonderful discussion about God and free will. They asked if they could return, and I said I would love nothing better. "Next time, I'll have lunch ready," I added.

I told a few ladies from my church about this wonderful visit. They informed me I was opening doors for evil to come into my life by letting two Mormon missionaries in my home. *Are you kidding me? A couple of twenty-year-olds trying to tell people about God?* I nearly started laughing. What could be so evil about two kids carrying out a scriptural mission while spending two hard years far away from home and family? I mean, how many of us ever spent two years away from our parents when we were in our late teens or early twenties—let alone not being able to have physical or verbal contact with them except at Christmas?

I didn't care what others said. When it came to religion and church, I had shifted. My time in Heaven shifted me. The visions and knowledge God had shared with me, implanted into my soul, had spiked my need and desire for knowledge. I thirsted for any and all information with a spiritual or religious basis, with a mission in mind: to focus on the essential spiritual points in common among all peaceful, love-based religions, rather than their man-made differences.

One evening I dreamed about my Angel, her wonderful aroma, and her loving attention fixed on my soul's welfare. The Aroma enveloped my room. I awoke and sat up in bed, which was still a difficult task. Why did I sit up? Because I could suddenly smell her? The room permeated with an angelic floral fragrance that lingered through the bedroom. I woke up my slumbering hubby, he agreed he could smell the aroma. As the aroma filled me, I remembered the peace and love I felt in Heaven. I felt protected again. "Do you smell her? Do you feel like you're in a meadow of flowers?" I asked. It was 3 a.m. and a man was almost certain to say anything to get me to shut up. "Yes" he repeated as I kept asking. "Can you see her sparkles of light, pointing toward the foot of the bed?"

No one needed to convince me: My Guardian Angel had returned to check on me. Perhaps she was back to admire her handiwork? She performed her job outstandingly well!

Back to the real world, and the Mormon missionaries. I found myself disagreeing with my church friends and their constrictive, hard-line attitudes: *If you don't follow Jesus Christ exactly as we say, then you won't be saved.*

Yeah . . . okay. This had always been a funny thought to me, but I was willing to overlook it. However, now it became difficult to tolerate. After being immersed in the Totality of Love when I tasted Eternity, a Totality that didn't seem to have any labels attached that I could readily make out (the clothes lover I am—I do take notice of labels), I knew the God I encountered would never say, "This way or the highway."

I searched for a more complete loving, spiritual place. I found myself searching for a better understanding of love and how it can be shared with everyone, here and now.

As a family, we continued to attend services at Valley Center Community Church. Pastor Sale had prayed so deeply for me the night of my accident, and then had visited almost daily at first, to offer me healing through the laying on of hands (which I felt even when deep in a coma). Pastor Sale said his plaintive prayer, while his hands heated the tissues of my abdomen; as he focused, a bright light would fill my mind's eye with peace and my chest cavity with warmth. I felt grateful to him. I admired him for his dedication to his congregation and most importantly to his beliefs. Several congregation members told me that my survival helped them with their walk. They had prayed for me for two months; to them, I was a testament of God's Love and His power of healing. Nobody needed to convince me of God's power, or just how much we are *not* in ultimate control of our lives.

Chapter 11

The Greatest Gift

Mother's Day, 2000

When Aaron and Nathan were younger, we shared a regular routine I called *gentlemen training.* Every week, we drove about twenty-five miles to the San Diego Wild Animal Park (now San Diego Zoo Safari Park). When a woman or girl approached the entrance doors (there were about twenty of them), my little gentlemen in training would open each door and hold it until the visitor passed through. After they opened one door, they rushed to the next door and held it open, until they covered all twenty-something doors. For their reward, they earned a fun day in the park, watching the animals run along this stretch of the San Pasqual Valley in the "Savannah" and "Serengeti" while enjoying ice cream. I'd also like to think they acquired a lifetime of good manners, which I still see every time we get together.

Back to Aaron, Nate, and the Wild Animal Park in a second . . .

About four months after I came home, in April 2000, Kris Reilly asked me to join her at a charity celebrity golf tournament. I still wasn't able to walk well yet or stand for too long, but Kris wanted to get me out of the house to visit with people and assist her at the tournament's registration tables. She knew I wouldn't be much help, but her goal was to help me return to my social volunteering ways. The tournament was full of professional athletes and faces familiar to San Diego County residents for a variety of reasons.

At the tournament, Kris introduced me to Steve Scholfield, an avid golfer and the popular, outspoken executive sports editor of the daily *The North County Times* and, before that, *The Blade-Tribune*.

To put it mildly (and in case you haven't noticed), we loved Steve in our household—and I always will love him.

I'd previously met Steve while at a sports event or charity function. He had covered my husband when he was a star quarterback at San Diego State, and they had since become good acquaintances. However, my memory was still partially blocked.

A few minutes later, when we were about twenty feet from each other, Steve called out from his golf cart: "Martha, great to see you! We all prayed for you. I'd love to write an article about you."

In front of all those big macho football players, now standing two and three deep at the registration check-in table I was working, I shouted to Steve, "An Angel accompanied me in Heaven! If you're gonna write the story, you'll have to include her." Even with a foggy mind, I wasn't afraid to say exactly what I wanted and meant!

At that moment, I fully expected Steve to point his golf cart in the opposite direction and play the eighteen holes backwards, just to get further away from this crazy, dinged-up blonde. That's not what happened. Instead, he drove over, gave me a hug, and looked into my eyes. "You just made it that much better," he said softly.

When I told my husband about the prospect of the article, he was so excited for me. He set up a lunch for Steve and us. Throughout the interview, that hubby of mine acted like the gleaming, proud poppa. He was so proud of me, and all that I had accomplished. I couldn't quite believe my good fortune: I had needed to hear his loving words so badly the past few months, and here they finally were. Gone were the series of "You can do it"s in coach-grunt. It felt so good hearing his praise as he chatted away about our new relationship. He shared with Steve about how we joked with people who hadn't seen me in awhile.

If they mentioned I looked skinny (I was very thin), we'd say I went on a crash diet, and I'd laugh and say, "I don't recommend my approach."

Great journalists are very opportunistic when it comes to asking the key question. Steve is also spiritual and intuitive. He felt our new joy with each other, which made him comfortable. He figured this was his opportunity. He wanted to know. Steve started asking about my Angel, I started talking, and he quickly became enthralled. I had promised God I would tell all about Him and the love I directly experienced in Heaven. That was my promise to the all-powerful, and I knew I must fulfill it. This arrangement, arrived at in the highest of places, is what made it possible for me to come back to mother my boys.

On Mother's Day, May 14, 2000, I received a wonderful present. Steve's brave article, "The Greatest Gift of All," covered the top quarter of *The North County Times* sports page. It recounted my recovery and determination, along with the blessed Mother's Day walk I wanted to take along the Wild Animal Park's Kilimanjaro Trail. It even quoted Valley Center High coach Rob Gilster, the one who found me on the road. "I didn't even recognize her," he said. "When the helicopter got there, they turned off their engine and I thought she was gone. I really think she did leave us, but through the grace of God, she came back."

My husband also was well quoted in the article. "Because she was an athlete, she was able to come through this sooner," he said. "Not once during this whole thing did she ask, 'Why did this happen to me'? She was always thinking, 'What do I have to do to get better?'"

It took some guts from all of us—my husband, Steve, and myself—but my Angel and I appeared "above the fold," as they refer to it in journalism—the lead story on the sports page on Mother's Day. It was one of the proudest moments in my life, because it brought together the things I have always cherished most: God, family, my boys, and sports.

Was my meeting with Steve at the golf tournament providence or coincidence? You decide. I know what I feel.

Later that day, my husband, boys, in-laws, and I walked the Kilimanjaro Trail at the San Diego Wild Animal Park. I will never forget the three miles of dusty, sweet-smelling sandstone and chaparral trail we walked. *No walk will ever compare to this,* I thought while walking with tears of joy. No walk has compared since.

Shortly after Mother's Day, on May 21, an old classmate of mine from high school wrote a letter to the editor, commending Steve on his wonderful Mother's Day story on me. Among other things, my old classmate wrote, "I grew up with Martha, and as amazing as her recovery is, it isn't surprising—she has always been one to match her grace and friendliness with a formidable inner resolve."

I hadn't spoken with or seen this guy since the middle of our senior year, twenty-three years earlier. I hadn't taken to reading the sports page, either, not even looking for my son Aaron's stats. That was the men in my family's territory, not mine. However, while Kris was driving me to therapy, she said laughingly, "Do you have a boyfriend on the side?"

"What?" Let's see . . . I'm fiercely loyal, fooling around on the side is not for me, I'm still physically disabled and clearing the fog from a head injury . . . "What boyfriend?" I asked.

"This guy who wrote the letter in the paper. He knows you really well."

I asked, "What's his name?"

Kris replied, "He must at least be an old boyfriend, I think it's Bob Yelling," not pronouncing his last name correctly. He had also changed his name from Robert. Not recognizing the butchered last name or the new first name, I had no idea who she was talking about.

I certainly knew a Robert Yehling. He'd been a friend of mine from school. A decade later, after some more twists and turns in our lives, and after more than thirty years of not seeing each other, we met at a mutual friend's gig at Hennessy's in Dana Point, about thirty miles up the coast of Oceanside. Remember I told you about my men and music? Wouldn't you know it? He did become my boyfriend; we fell in love.

After the article and Bob's response, Palomar Hospital's public relations department contacted me. They had read a thank-you letter I'd sent to the Emergency Trauma unit, and asked if I'd be interested in helping the hospital with PR. "You saved my life. I'll do anything for you. Just let me know," I said.

I'd do the same today. I'm available to them for life, as long as I can clear my work schedule. I'm theirs for the asking. That's my version of paying it forward.

I was asked if I'd come down and sign a release. A few weeks later in the mail, I received a large post card. It read, "Palomar Medical Center's Trauma & Emergency Department—We are your only Trauma Center from Rancho Santa Fe to Julian, Temecula to Rancho Bernardo. Fifty years of caring for the community." Smack on the card was a photo of me from my competitive track days, sprinting with those long strides I'd love to have back some day. There was also the caption, "I'm alive today because of Palomar's Trauma Center." The front cover caption read, "When You Have No Time to Spare."

I hoped this was not the first time they would ask me to help.

I battled daily with trying to figure out why I came back, other than to continue my mothering. I needed another purpose for my life. The whole literature thing was new to me; I had a need for reading, but my book tastes had completely changed. I used to love Robert Ludlum and spy thrillers in general. Now, if I didn't gain some type of meaningful or useful knowledge in a book, I had no interest in reading it.

Also, it was taxing not to be able to drive; the boys and I had always been on the move. I was one of those moms that filled the car with boys and hauled them to the beach, jumped on the trampoline, went to movies, roller-skating, water parks, laser tag, or basketball games—whatever we could find in North San Diego County. More often than not, this tomboy who liked to wear dresses jumped into the fray, especially at the beach. I could hear my Grand Mary's voice in my head, *Idle hands are the devil's workshop.* I figured there must be some wisdom within that saying, so I kept my boys busy. Since I couldn't drive and had no purposeful reading material, I started renting movies for entertainment.

There was a video rental place across the street. I felt comfortable driving that little distance. The boys and I would zip over and I would rent the same movies over and over again. Nate would gently touch my arm, looking at me with his concerned eleven-year-old eyes, which were being forced into becoming the mature eyes of a twenty five-year-old. "*Mom, you've seen that one,*" he'd say. Aaron became frustrated that I wouldn't remember having rented it and refuse to watch it *again* with me.

What were my sons talking about? Odd. They insisted we'd seen the movie—more than once, more than twice—but clearly, we hadn't seen it. So I thought. The lady at the store would just smile at me when I'd pleaded with the boys, "No, I have not seen *that* movie before." She'd ring it up again, in some cases for the third or fourth time. My memory was certainly not back!

My multiple viewing habits finally dawned on me the third time I watched *Stigmata* with Nate curled up next to me. I looked at him with amazement as he quoted the dialogue line for line, but this time I remembered. In shock, I looked at him. "I remember this part!" I exclaimed. I proceeded to tell him how the rest of the movie would play out.

Aaron also noticed. "Thank God," he said, deeply relieved.

My boys were so strong. Not only did they have a mom who returned in a new, weaker body, but she also had a new personality. I held little or no short-term memory, I was too weak and short of breath to do our usual horseplay, and my lighthearted personality was now too serious. I felt so blessed by God, yet so challenged by my circumstances (physically and spiritually) that I needed to stay focused. Simply said, I no longer possessed the sense of humor that had always been a big part of me. I was becoming way too churchie. (Well, thankfully, it was temporary; I don't know how I could live with that ultra-serious girl were she around today.)

I had always told my boys, "Every time you point a finger at someone, there are three fingers pointing right back at you. You must never judge other people." This was our family's hard and fast rule. Years before, I had left the community church because the old pastor (at that time) told me I was a single mom, raising my boys myself. I took offense to this. One reason was that the pastor was dead wrong. It happened that my husband worked broadcasting football games on Sundays, which left me alone at morning services. In the pastor's narrow eyes, working on Sundays was blasphemous. Funny—the way I saw it, he also worked on Sunday, just a different job.

Once again I had to leave the church. This time it had nothing to do with the pastor; I loved him, I just needed a wider understanding. I needed new companionship, so I decided to join a group of girlfriends at a Bible study. The group was a conglomerate of ladies from several different churches and faiths; a variety I felt would breed knowledge and openness. That attracted me. I happily joined a group of about eight women at the home of Sherry Ness, for studies by Beth Moore.

Now I found my purposeful reading material, but it became very difficult and overwhelming trying to read so much and put together a full understanding of my unique experience, and my new perspective on life. We shared our views at Beth's studies once a week while the kids were in class. I spent the rest of 2000 and the first part of 2001 completing four of Beth's studies: *Jesus the One and Only*; *Breaking Free*; *A Heart like His*; and *A Woman's Heart*. The studies typically ran ten weeks, but our group speed through in about six weeks on each.

After all this Bible reading and deep thought, my search not yet complete, I decided I was ready to move on. I was now driving and ready to drive into my next adventure in life.

The Norbulingka Institute of preserving Tibetan Culture, outside Dharamsala, India. A school where selected artists (a great honor) will spend ten to twenty years perfecting their craft.

Padmasambhava Monastery. Once a year butter sculptures are displayed. These are amazing pieces of colorful, lovely, intricately carved artwork.

Receiving a prayer bracelet from a Buddhist monk outside the Bodhi Tree in Bodh Gaya.

Above: White water rafting Himalayan snow melt waters on the Ganges north of Rishikesh.

Left: Our guide with the best Cheshire Cat smile ever. He led us to a blissful day of adventure.

My little Hindu friends. Many of these boys were street kids or unattended.
We visited their spiritual place, the Ramakrishna & Kali Temple, which was
built in 1847.

My big lil' friends: my son Nate, son Aaron, and daughter-in-law Amy. I am
blessed to have them in my heart and life.

The 2013 Missoula Montana Half Marathon

I still enjoy thinking of that final kick through the finish line in Missoula.

The Taj Mahal in Agra. The city has clear air because there is no industry allowed to protect this wonderful architectural marvel.

Chapter 12

Waves, Work, and Wisdom

When Summer 2000 arrived, I couldn't wait to hit the beach and show my boys I was back to my old self. Nine months after the accident, on a smoldering July day in Pauma Valley, the boys and I piled everyone into our Suburban and set off for my hometown of Carlsbad, an hour away. My old friend, the Pacific Ocean, was calling.

Some of my friends spent a week or two each summer at the Best Western Hotel, located just down the beach from Army-Navy Academy, where I spent many childhood summers learning to swim and playing in the ocean. When we arrived, we trekked down the public stair access to the beach, a full workout for me, and saw beach canopies. Beneath them were a cluster of boys, boogie boards, fins, coolers, and Tommy Bahama beach chairs, along with my friends Kris, Margaret, and Pam, and their husbands. While the guys were bodysurfing, after resting and catching my breath, I set down my cane and asked Aaron to help me to the water.

Once I entered the ocean, I felt like a mermaid, at home in my element. It brought back a great memory of swimming a quarter-mile out to the kelp beds with my friends, Cindy Kison and Lisa Weibrecht—right after the *Jaws* movie release. As we moved closer to the kelp beds, I would taunt them with the soundtrack of the approaching shark. *Dunt da dunt da da da . . .*

They squealed as I made fin motions with my hand in the water, laughing hysterically. Really, why would an able-bodied shark want to mess with my fun?

There were no sharks, then or now. Just my overwhelming joy at being in the ocean again. Kris's husband, Russ, and Pam's husband, Mike, worried about how I would fare in the waves, but I felt pretty safe because Mike was a physical therapist and Russ was a stocky athlete. Plus, I am eminently comfortable in the ocean. To me, it is the very cocoon of God's Love (an analogy you often hear from surfers as well, especially when they're riding in the tube, the hollow part of the wave). The boys and I played in the waves while everyone fussed about my safety, both the ladies from the beach and the men from the water. There was no need to worry. I was a big kid, full of childlike glee.

Soon, a body surfing competition ensued . . . and I was the instigator. *To hell with them wondering if I can or not . . . let me ride this!* Just like the old days, if you were on my wave, I would cut you off. Soon, the guys figured out that I might be frail on land, but in the water, I ruled. *I'm home, I'm me, I'm so happy. I feel strong.*

All too soon, the day ended. As we drove home to Pauma Valley, all I could think about was overcoming my fear of driving and taking the boys and myself to the beach as often as possible. However, while driving serpentine Highway 76 with the boys' banter in the back, the noise from the radio, motorcycles zipping between the lanes, and RVs heading out to the desert with motorcycles in tow, I thought of the boy from rehab. All he had wanted to experience was a desert adventure; now, he would live in a wheelchair forever. My back and neck muscles clenched with apprehension. *How will I ever be able to make this drive on my own?*

The boys and I spent most of that summer at home in the pool. Unfortunately, I was dealing with another drawback as significant as my fear of driving: My insurance had run low and I had been cut loose from physical therapy. When David told me it was time for me to leave the nest, he took me to the 24 Hour Fitness I belonged to and walked me through some exercises.

These included sitting on a medicine ball to improve my balance, and different weight machines to strengthen my arms and core. It took me only a few times to realize I couldn't do it without him; climbing up the single flight of stairs was too much for me. I was terrified of falling down.

We talked about it, and found an alternative: water aerobics.

I loved the water aerobics ladies at the YMCA. They ranged in age from one thirty-year-old, to me at forty, to the majority of the crew, which were in their late sixties and seventies. While most of the ladies stayed in the shallow end, I needed to venture into the deep end because of my height. We laughed about it. We had to wear banana yellow flotation devices around our waists—the same color as the short school bus, if you catch my drift. And yes, I felt that awkward, because the water had always been my strength. I'm still this way; just add water and I'm good to go. But don't ask me to do any of that dry land weight pumping.

The holiday season quickly arrived. Almost a year had passed since the accident. One day at a Bible study, which was held at Sherry and Tom's, for whom I'd worked many years at Bates Nut Farm. I decorated the property with homemade scarecrows for the annual Harvest Fest and Thanksgiving season. During Christmas, I helped with the holiday decorating. I merchandised the store's homey giftware, sold the many candy and nut goodies, and gave educational talks to students on school field trips. Outside, I trimmed trees and built various displays.

At the Bible study, Tom asked, "What date should I put you back on the work schedule?" He followed his words with a big, beautiful smile.

Wow! I hadn't thought about that. "I'm not sure I'm ready. I want to be . . . "

Beyond that, I was speechless, intimidated, and overwhelmed by the confidence Tom showed me. It was more than I felt in myself. Even now, many years later, it brings me to tears writing about his incredible gesture.

Tom and Sherry knew I wasn't physically or mentally strong enough to work in the same capacity as before, but they hired me anyway to put price tags on the products. I sat on a stool for two to three hours daily, which was all I could manage. The work filled me with holiday joy, but I was also discouraged. I realized my mind was still foggy and my body still weak. I needed to be taught everything from pricing to inventory, and after years of merchandising this should have been second nature. In addition, I had such difficulty remembering everyone's names, customers and employees alike. This drove me nuts because I had worked with them for years. My new daily saying became, *I used to be able to . . .*

Still, I knew how far I'd come, and thanked God for all of it.

The beautifully decorated Christmas trees at Bates reminded me of the day at Scripps, when my wheelchair brigade and I decorated (haha) a cheap, homely synthetic tree with the most horrendous ornaments I'd ever seen. They were worse than the discarded ornaments at Big Lots or Salvation Army!

I decided the Bible Study group and I needed to change that. I asked the group to donate enough decorations to fill the tree. Also, we needed to have a specific design and theme. That's my thing, design and decoration! I asked the girls to bring non-breakable ornaments within a particular color scheme to our study the following week.

I got a ride down to Scripps, bringing along my friend Joie who had just been a patient there. We returned to share our victory of walking. Joie had an NDE while undergoing a surgery that had complications. His had not been positive! I saw the fear on his face as he spoke with me sharing his experience. My heart leapt out toward him, wanting to let him know it doesn't have to be that way next time.

When we delivered the decorations, we arrived during the middle of a meeting. When I knocked on the door, my occupational therapist (the great guy, Peter) came out. At first, he didn't recognize me. The last time he'd seen me, I was quite a sight, with messy unwashed hair, no makeup, homely workout clothes, and a wheelchair. Now, I stood there wearing a nice outfit, my hair highlighted and blown dry, and my make up meticulously applied.

Light glowed in his eyes. "You're not that same woman who couldn't bake that cake out of a box," he said teasingly. He was amazed by my progress.

All I could do was smile. I felt so blessed with the goodness of life, for the blessing that God had given to me.

However, I still felt conflicted by one small thing: Which home did I *really* want to occupy now? I longed to return to the simple harmony and love I heard, smelled, and felt in Heaven. I wanted to go back! The best way for me to get close, I thought, was to stay involved in my church and my quest for spiritual knowledge. I wanted to share this with my family. I kept up my Bible study with my girlfriends, but wished I could find that same degree of spiritual nourishment in a church community.

I opted to volunteer at the church bookstore. I was finally at work again, real work. Wow! I was actually running the cash register again, where, to my astonishment, I realized my math skills had diminished, but I wasn't sure what aspects I'd left on Middle Grade Road during my accident.

One day, while picking up Nate from school, I talked to my friends Colleen and Chris. I told them I was lacking some of my old math skills, but I wasn't sure which skills. What could they suggest? Since I had volunteered at the school for years, they had something special in mind. They took me to the principal's office—for a far different reason than the few times I was sent there in high school. "Let's set you up for the test we give everyone who applies for teachers' aide positions," the principal offered.

Chris explained to me that the test would reveal my new shortcomings in math and writing. Sure enough, my mental evaluation showed my head injury had damaged my skills in fractions and making change, as well as many writing skills.

Later, at home, I talked with one of my family members about the test. "On the test, there was this funny thing: the number three, a slash, and then a four. Also, a dot and a number. What do you suppose those are?"

"The first thing is three-quarters."

"Three-quarters of what?"

"A whole number . . . and the dot and number signify a percentage for change." My family member drew it out to show me. "Is that what they were?"

"Exactly."

I picked up first-, third-, and fifth-grade-level booklets at a teacher's bookstore. In just a short period time, I found myself able to understand math and make change at the bookstore. The old Virginia Slims cigarette ad and commercial slogan, "You've come a long way, baby," became my new self-motivating theme song.

I loved working in that bookstore. It offered me the peace, joy and quiet to read books about God and spirit. I didn't even have to buy them! After being immersed in Heaven's magnificent beauty, realizing that everything in life is connected, I needed to see it described in books. In Heaven, I saw that life is energy, and that this energy is within us, and in every cell of all life. However, I was having a very difficult time finding it in spiritual literature.

These thoughts racked my mind daily. However, I was afraid if I shared them with more friends in Valley Center and Pauma Valley, someone would come along, add a stiff little white jacket to my wardrobe, and haul me off to a room with padded walls. I could still hear that nurse at Scripps Rehab Center warning me, *If you tell anyone, they will never let you out of here.*

I needed to find an outlet, where people would be willing and wanting to hear about God's Love. My mind kept screaming at me, *You made a promise to the Almighty to tell everyone about His Love.* I knew then my mission would be to relate God's similarities of Love. The words "a taste of eternity" had been playing in my mind and heart since the moment I awoke from my coma.

I looked around the bookstore shelves, and then it dawned on me: *A Taste of Eternity.* I needed to write a book about my accident, my new life, and what it all meant.

New Beginnings—

Rediscovering Myself

As my body strengthened, I realized that I needed to strengthen my mental focus as well. I needed to acquire knowledge so that I could get back to work to help pay the $850,000 we carried on our credit for the eighteen months it took the insurance company to review our bill. In other words, our credit was ruined.

I also knew from my basal skull fracture that I had in fact suffered a brain injury, the full extent of which I didn't know. One thing we know about traumatic brain injuries: It sometimes takes years to gain a complete picture of the damage we suffered, the effects on our lives that resulted, and the types of long-term damage that could either impact the rest of our lives, or recur later in life in ways such as dementia or early onset Alzheimer's. Unfortunately, no one seemed to have that answer in 2001. TBI was still little known or understood. If you hit your head hard, you suffered a concussion. End of story. Therefore, TBI was never discussed socially, and there were few books or counseling programs. There certainly weren't any TBI recovery workbooks developed from direct experience, such as the wonderful *After*

Brain Injury: Telling Your Story, which TBI expert Barbara Sta-hura wrote after her husband's near fatal motorcycle accident.

However, there was a daily reminder that I was still far from mentally complete: the boys' growing frustration when I rented the same movie over and over again, certain I had never seen it before. It wasn't funny anymore.

I was constantly asking myself, *Why am I here?* On top of that, I had a new odd drive and desire to constantly learn more. Not that I walked around every day saying this to myself, or anyone else for that matter, but I was drawn to improving myself, and my memory. What did I enjoy? In what activities or situations did I currently have a good understanding, or the confidence I could handle them? *What can I possibly do to help with $850,000 in bills?*

I looked at my earliest fallback position. In the early 1980s, during my college days in Northern Idaho, I'd been a Real Estate Appraiser for the Kootenai County Tax Assessor. I was part of a team that consisted of several fifty- and sixty-year-old men, along with two young women in their early twenties hired to fill a job quota. I was one of those women. My equally youthful colleague, Lynn, and I seemed to get the more interesting assignments. While most of the men appraised nearby homes and properties in Coeur d'Alene, we would draw the odd jobs on the backside of Lake Coeur d'Alene, the backside of Kootenai County. In the early 1980s (to this California girl), it was like driving into the outback.

I remember visiting one property to appraise new additions. When I arrived, I saw a yellow school bus with a stove pipe-chimney hooked up to it and curtains in the windows. Next to the bus, I saw a concrete basement structure with a front door. Mind you, this happened in the dead of winter, when it was sub-freezing. I knocked on the door and was greeted by a double-barreled sawed-off shotgun and, behind it, a burly man. Blanket partitions separated the rooms. "I'm here to appraise your additions from your permit," I said, my voice shaking.

The man's wife ran out of the school bus and tried to calm him down. She put her hand on the barrel of the shotgun and pointed it downward, while I tried to take a couple steps backwards. Like that was going to help any. My eyes opened wide, like a close-up we usually see of the girl about to meet her maker in a horror film. "I can clearly see none of your improvements have happened yet. I have nothing for my report," I said.

I walked quickly to the car—and bolted.

Later, it occurred to me why the man greeted me so "warmly" and why his wife burst out of the school bus, obviously their present home: They saw the official county seal painted on the car's door panel. I'm sure they thought it was a police shield.

This wasn't even my most far-fetched appraisal experience. One morning walking into the office, I overheard two of the men discussing the latest assignment to cross our desk. The shorter man, of Italian descent, said, "I can't do it; they'd never let me on the property. You should go. You're a big, white Norwegian Viking-looking guy. You might even intimidate them."

Then they turned—and there I was. They looked back at each other and said, "She's perfect. Martha . . . Brookhart, isn't that a German name?"

I smiled, not knowing what their conversation was about. "It could be . . ."

"What could be more perfect than a six-foot blonde-haired, blue-eyed, athletic twenty-something female with a German last name?" the short Italian asked.

They scurried upstairs and talked to the manager. Next thing I knew, I was handed the file. All three gathered around and gave me a breakdown on where I was going. "Do you know what a magazine is?" one asked.

Do you fools know you're talking to a model? "Sure. *Vogue. Glamour.* I *am* studying fashion merchandising," I said. "I *have* modeled."

They chuckled and told me how to get to my destination and who I would be looking for—Tom Metzger. They said his name in a strange way, like he was the bogeymen or something. His name meant nothing to me. Then they described their version of a magazine: a railroad car-sized metal storage unit that typically contains ammunition. "Do you think you can do this?" the manager asked.

I looked directly at him. "A bunch of white guys? Of course I can."

I drove onto the property. The buildings were arranged in a U-shaped pattern. Instead of going to a particular building, I stopped the car in the middle of the gravel central area. The set-up was in the middle of a dense evergreen forest north of Coeur d'Alene, towards Sandpoint. It looked a lot more like an organized compound than a scattering of outbuildings around a house.

When I got out of the car, two bald-headed young men wearing black boots approached me. "What do you want?" they asked suspiciously.

"I'm here to see Tom Metzger."

They looked at each other, stepped away, and mumbled. They walked off toward one of the buildings.

The next thing I knew, I was talking to a nice man who took me on a tour of the property. He even helped take measurements with my tape. It didn't feel odd, nor did I feel threatened. Quite the opposite. The man thoroughly enjoyed measuring buildings with a young California girl. We even discussed North San Diego County, where my hometown is located. He said he used to live in Fallbrook, about 20 miles away. I told him about growing up in Carlsbad.

When I got back to the office, the men started buzzing around me. "Did you get to go into the magazine?" one asked.

"Yes. I saw three magazines," I said. "But I didn't get to go inside."

"Did you see Metzger?"

"Yes. He even helped me take my measurements. He was a nice man."

They glanced at each other, and then looked at me. "Martha, do you have any idea who he is?"

"No. You just told me to go to his property and appraise it, and I did."

By now, the men were smiling and laughing, but they also had concerned looks, as if to say, *We could've hurt our girl.* "Martha, Metzger. Tom Metzger."

I shrugged.

"Tom Metzger is the head of the White Aryan Resistance. You know, the big dog of the KKK?"

I flipped my hands out. "Oh, thanks you guys!" I said, exasperated. "But don't worry. I told you I would get it done, and I did."

From these experiences I knew I had the fortitude to deal with almost any situation that would present itself. On a far less perilous note, I also had good experience with home loan terminology. I had acquired an interest in houses through osmosis. I'd spent six years decorating for Bates Nut Farm, focusing mainly on home interiors. Then there was the fifteen years of maintaining a well decorated home for my family. So I knew my easiest path back into the workplace would run through homes.

I had two years prior enrolled in a real estate class at the local junior college, to work on my memory skills. It was difficult but fun, and I enjoyed both the interaction with classmates and the mental challenge.

One day on campus, I ran into a group of students who had suffered head trauma at some point, which resulted in brain damage with varying degrees of severity. This motley but happy crew became my new friends. They met in a lounge area set aside for them, which happened to be near my real estate classroom. This section of the campus had special therapists to help these students with classes, jobs, meals, and finances, or whatever else they needed.

I began meeting with a few of my new peeps, as I called them, almost every day, even though my real estate class only met twice a week. I enjoyed the conversations. Sometimes, we talked about their math or reading assignments. At other times, we talked about their home life, friends, and how they sometimes felt ostracized by the rest of society. I liked practicing with them, helping them out as I could. Besides being my once-again sociable self—"She" had gone MIA for fifteen months after the accident—I was seeing if I would like to become trained as some type of therapy assistant. I still wish I had done this, I would be happy in a career helping others, giving of myself.

The tables had turned: Now I felt I could help others, rather than being on the receiving end. As I look back, I see that this was the beginning of me coming out of my shell and setting my feet forward to be proactive, not self-protective. I was becoming the new me.

I was fortunate to gain a two-sided advantage from meeting with this group. First, in a roundabout way, I received free counseling from aides and therapists. Also, I received reverse therapy from my peeps, because they shared so many of my frustrations about memory, walking funny, and the looks strangers gave us. Most importantly, they also knew what it felt like to not be the same person on the outside even though you felt the same on the inside. When overcome with frustration, some would unleash a verbal hurricane. They'd complain about something, and I would think *Ah ha that's right I feel the same . . . Voilà!* Instant therapy, and I didn't even have to ask for it.

Yet, as I watched them, I noticed that they never gave up. They smiled for the most part, and carried themselves with so much dignity. They gave me that extra *ummfffff* I needed. When I'd think my real estate class or working on the computer was becoming too difficult, I'd think again. From this group came a saying I repeat to myself to this day: *Do you remember that guy that quit? No . . . that's because nobody does.* I learned to never give up, even when I wanted to run and hide from the crowd.

Being in the crowd was part of the new me. I loved God; he was my Heavenly Father. I had been raised with this belief at St. Michael's Episcopal Church in Carlsbad. I had been a Christian, by my own choosing since my freshman year in high school, and by my parents' choosing, since I was a baptized into the church as a baby. Now God wanted me to be part of his crowd, but to do so in a different way. This was part of our "Deal," my promise that resulted in my returning to my babies. My pops held his Christianity dear to his heart, but he didn't Bible-thump or quote scripture. He didn't trust people who quoted verses at one another, and neither did I. I still don't. Pops always said, "It doesn't matter what other people hear from you, it matters what God hears from you." He was the first person I told about going to "The Light," of being with God. He was the perfect man, in his daughter's eyes. I like to say, "There are only two men I know of who walk on water and they are both my father—my pops and my Heavenly Father." I had a deep desire to make them both proud of me.

My dad still attended weekly Sunday services at St. Michael's. The members loved my dad, so they stood by him during my coma. He didn't like visiting the hospital . . . any hospital. He visited church instead. There, the "Daughters of the King," the St. Michael's Church ladies group, placed me on their prayer list. We're not talking about saying a few prayers and moving on. They prayed for me twenty-four hours daily for two full months, taking shifts. They put in some serious kneel time for me. I had known many of these ladies since childhood, but more importantly, they loved my dad. He shared his excitement with the ladies when I first woke and told him about the light.

(As I learned later, the prayer circle surrounding my wellbeing extended far beyond my childhood church. During the time I was in my coma, I was placed on prayer lists all over San Diego County, as well as a few lists worldwide, including a Canadian convent, and a Catholic monastery in Italy.)

Now, a question nagged at me: What do I get Mr. Perfect for his eightieth birthday? On March 6, 2001, I had just the answer: the first, raw outline of what became my working title, *A Taste of Eternity*, and eventually, *The Fragrance of Angels*. I started writing primarily to gain a deeper understanding of what had happened to me, and how my experience continued to seep into my everyday life. Pops had instilled the knowledge-building qualities that kept me going, fighting for more understanding and wisdom, so I was pleased to share it and dedicate the story to him. It was a small package, only a few pages, but wrapped in pretty paper. When he opened it, his eyes filled with tears. As I watched him, something welled up in me, too: a growing desire to publicly share my time in Heaven. After Pops told the Daughters of the King about his birthday gift, we agreed that I needed to share this story "publicly" with them first, at the church of my youth. It meant everything to him.

It turned into one of the greatest experiences of my new life— and the beginning of school and church talks and discussions to which I continue to be invited to this day. I hope it never ends. Where there are receptive souls, hearts, and minds, there I will be to tell my story.

That afternoon, I walked into a full house at the St. Michael's reception center. I nervously smiled to the crowd of ladies I had known and respected since I was a bratty kid, women like Dorothy Krepps, Pat Miller, Ginny Unanue, and the cookie ladies, the Sunday volunteers I had probably annoyed as a little girl running through the congregational hall. I was supposed to be a lady, quiet and unseen, walking and not running. I never saw that particular page in the etiquette playbook.

Suddenly, I was unsure of what to say. If you know me, you know *that* doesn't happen often! After a very long couple of seconds, I decided to open up and let God take over. All of a sudden, the words just started to flow out. I told them how I passed over and into the Light, of being with an Angel, of meeting the Trinity, undergoing a life review, and the beauty of Heaven. I shared the perfection of Heaven, and how I came back unafraid of death . . . and they shouldn't be afraid, either. I told them more than I had ever told anyone about my experience.

Just as the words came to me, they also ended. I'm not sure how I knew, but my story was finished and it was time to stop. I looked out at the crowd, which also included a few men. Many were wide-eyed, their mouths open; tears rolled down the cheeks of many others. They gave me a warm round of applause. I quickly walked to my dad's side as the pastor tied together everything I said with biblical references. Not my favorite thing, but the pastor did it tastefully, and it all connected to what I had said. Suddenly, instead of the cookie ladies shooing away the little girl, they extended platters of cookies to her. Hey . . . works for me!

After my talk, I realized that I needed more of the feeling of community that I grew up with, something in addition to my Beth Moore study girls. My baby Nate, now twelve and maturing in his own beliefs, started attending a youth group at Ridgeview Church. One Sunday, I gave his church a try. They seemed more hip and welcoming of all types of Christians, and I liked that. It didn't matter to them how much you knew, could quote, or how new or experienced a Christian you were. They welcomed all people. I wanted to attend and be part of a church that sought out the similarities in people without trying to mold them into a certain prescribed, cookie-cutter Stepford Wives model. I've never liked flowered dresses with white Peter Pan collars, and my friends will tell you how I respond to being told I need to act or think a certain way.

I was having difficulty with church groups that kept telling me if I didn't praise God in their particular fashion, then I was doing it wrong, or I wasn't a good Christian. This hurt me, deeply. I wanted everyone to have that unconditional, *Agape* Love I had shared in Heaven. Didn't they understand this is, after all, why we go to church, temple, the Mosque, or a beach park service with our friends, or why we pray and meditate? Whatever happened to Jesus's teaching, "Where two or more are gathered, there I will be . . . ?" Well, I just quoted scripture—but it's a verse that should resonate with universal freedom of worship rather than a set dogma or service time, just as its speaker intended. I was still filled with that high intensity and vibration of how we're supposed to love one another, and I wasn't finding it. Some folks said you cannot die and come back, this is not possible for followers of Christ, my answer was, "Well I'm Christian, and it happened."

I realized, trying to find the new me, that I needed to forge another approach to find people who may understand my thoughts. I figured if I new more about NDEs, it would help. I started reading *Embraced by the Light*, the twenty-year best seller Kris had given me in the hospital. Reading this small, 159-page book made me feel whole, like I wasn't a crackpot. As I read each page, I realized that Betty Eadie, a complete stranger, was writing details (twenty pages' worth) that matched part of my NDE experience. She wrote them evocatively, with emotion, which affirmed to me that she really lived the experience. At first, I was stunned to see these similarities in print, but then it really warmed my heart. *Embraced by the Light* took me again to the question that kept nagging me: *Why do the vast majority of religions and spiritual beliefs consider their way to be the only right way?*

I began searching for some answers of my own. I found statements by other people who had near-death experiences that shared the same or similar descriptions of God. I found them documented over many centuries, from different cultures, lifestyles, religions, and spiritualities. I saw it in words and in medieval art. As I discovered more of these statements, it fueled my drive to relate these similarities. I had to find the answers. I have to say it was driving me a bit nuts.

Nate's new junior high youth group, whom I called his "Bible Buddies," asked me to share some of my story. I was pleased, but I wanted the parents to feel assured and comfortable, so I found scripture to back up some of my points. Like I said, this is not my style, but if it was going to help and convey the message, then I would resort to what Bob describes to his writing students as "the Mary Poppins approach"—a spoonful of sugar helps the medicine go down. My story is the medicine; the scripture is the spoonful of context the parents can connect to my story.

We met in the open room the kids reserved for their weekly get-togethers, a hip place where they held everything from concerts and Bible studies to parties. There were more girls than boys, which made it easy for me to relate a moral of the story. I stressed lessons of forgiveness, both offering and (most of all) asking for it. I shared with them how, during my life review, I had to wholly experience how I made another person feel—including how deeply I hurt them. I shared how I had inadvertently hurt a girl's feelings way back when I was their age in junior high. I hadn't thought about it then or since, but I had been cruel to her and had never asked for forgiveness by her or God. Guess what? I got to experience how she felt in 3-D surround-sound IMAX Technicolor. I told the group that they would serve themselves well by learning to ask for forgiveness. I still stress the importance of asking for forgiveness or going to confession, as I did to the sixty-plus kids in my friend Kathy Eckert's CCD class at St. Stephen's Catholic Church in 2014.

As I talked to Nate's youth group, I saw the pride and happiness on his face. It was like I was *his* kid; it was his turn for sharing, and I was his pet he brought in for show and tell. He was ecstatic. I was overjoyed that he was so proud of me. I saw the love on his face . . . wow, what a sight.

By Spring 2001, my life was beginning to regrow and rejuvenate. I started to feel almost back to normal, active in all sorts of volunteer activities, and fulfilling my drive to constantly learn more, to keep my brain engaged. I'd learned that, every time you study and acquire knowledge, it increases the electrical impulses between your brain synapses, and actually increases overall capacity. In addition, Palomar Pomerado hospital began utilizing me as a featured former patient and spokesperson for general promotion and fundraising activities. This included a feature article on me in their oversized tabloid-style magazine, *Well Spring,* entitled "Saving Martha." It aptly captured the medical part of my story, and is worth revisiting:

Martha Halda knows firsthand about the important work done by the trauma team at Palomar Medical Center. She knows because they saved her life.

Two years ago, Martha was on her way to pick up her son at school in (Valley Center), a rural area of North County. Coming over a hill, she was blinded by the sun and lost control of her vehicle, which ran off the road and flipped end over end. Thrown from the car, Martha sustained injuries so severe that she had to be revived three times in the helicopter that transported her to Palomar Medical Center.

With broken ribs, punctured lungs, multiple fractures to her leg and pelvis, and injuries to her diaphragm, liver, bladder and spleen, Martha required the immediate and focused attention of Palomar's experienced trauma team. Doctors, nurses, medical technicians, x-ray technicians and other staff worked together to save Martha.

Trauma surgeon David Cloyd, M.D., repaired numerous internal injuries during an incredible eight hours of surgery. She woke up briefly after surgery, able to move her limbs and demonstrate her determination. Seven weeks under deep sedation allowed her injuries to heal.

After leaving the hospital, Martha was transferred to a rehabilitation center where she learned to walk again. When Martha was sent home to continue her recovery, her first stop was Palomar's Trauma Unit to thank the many people who had worked so hard to save her life.

Today, Martha Halda grows stronger each day and enjoys walking, golfing, and water aerobics.

"I'm here today because of the God-given talents of Dr. Cloyd and all the staff," she says. "Some trauma teams would have given up; I thank God they didn't give up on me. The doctors and nurses at Palomar are angels on earth. They saved my life . . . they could save yours, too."

On July 30, my fellow Bible study girlfriend decided she wanted to help me fulfill my promise that I would tell of God's Love. Kelly Crews is a vivacious, self-motivated, and focused woman who helped her husband run a successful home development company. She wanted to love and assist other women to find their own strengths and value. We shared this mission in common. She decided to be my advocate. She started writing about me and applying for my story to be part of a short-lived network television show called *Beyond Chance*. I will forever cherish her friendship and the proactive way she helped to get my story out there. The story wasn't accepted but her diligence in trying to get my story out there was encouraging and spurred me on. I started hearing "a taste of eternity" more often running through my mind; it sort of danced and sparkled the way the flowers and scents did in Heaven.

Meanwhile, Nate's excitement about his youth group made me equally excited to be a part of the congregation. I attended a few ladies getaway retreats and found that I enjoyed their company. They were so good at making me feel welcome and part of the group. I wanted to give more to this church, but what could I do that focused on God and His Love, come from my heart, and also involve the skills and talents God gave me?

I turned to what I know—decorating. My good friend, Cathey Anderson, picked up on it, and encouraged me to decorate the church for Christmas. What an honor, to dress one of God's homes!

Ridgeview Church sits at the edge of Valley Center, atop a hill overlooking Pauma Valley, with a bird's eye view of Palomar Mountain. When you take the time to really look at the view, you don't want to blink, for fear you may miss something—perhaps a misty, stretched cloud, a hawk soaring in a circular current, or the fresh smell of orange blossoms in full bloom filling the air with their sweetness. Yep, I like it in God's country.

The church building is large, set in an auditorium style without an altar but with a center stage. Cathey knew I wasn't a decorate-by-committee type of girl; I liked to work by myself. This is one of my vanities I need to work on, but I believe I have great taste and a good eye for special decoration and color. Plus, I'm much faster at seeing the big picture and mentally envisioning the final product when I don't have to collaborate.

I started organizing my stash of decorating materials and sorting through the half-dozen large boxes of mix-and-match stuff this new church had stored. As I twisted and fluffed all the swags, bows, ornaments, and wreaths, a man walked onto the stage and starting playing Christmas music on the keyboard. I was being treated to my very own concert! I stopped for a break and chatted with him. A few minutes later, an old friend, Lisa, walked in. Lisa was a welcome face from my youth in Carlsbad. She had been part of my sister Katie's group of junior and high school friends, and I hadn't seen her in more than twenty years. I squealed like a junior high girl, and so did she. We were so surprised to see each other. As it turned out, her husband John was performing my wonderful private concerto.

We caught up quickly. John told me he attended the Army-Navy Academy. "Do you remember Ray Brookhart?" I asked.

He proceeded to tell me a story of how my dad assisted his mother with the tuition that she couldn't afford. Pops made sure

John was covered as long as needed. This is a story every woman would want to know about her father's kindness, a story I would never have known if I had not volunteered to give my time—time I had because God made it possible for me to live again. This incredible story about my father was another example of God's providence. It was so perfectly orchestrated.

When I got home each night, I gradually whittled down the mountain of Christmas cards I needed to send out. Prior to 1999, we sent simple, Hallmark-style Christmas cards. In 2000, I wrote a special thank-you message that took me three days. My written note for 2001 didn't take nearly as long, but its message spoke of the things we give to another, rather than things we purchase or possess:

Christmas Spirit is not something you can run down to the mall and pick up. It's only that 'something' you give away as you offer a hug or smile. However, sometimes you may be lucky enough to be on the receiving end of this wonderful gift of the Christmas Spirit.

Last year and this year, we were just that lucky! It's December 18th. I've been home from the hospital for one year today. My, how much can change in one year!

Christmas Spirit: this is truly something our community has a lot of. From a moment of silence for me at the football game the night of the accident to the many, many meals brought lovingly to our home for months . . . the ride home from the hospital sent by Mark's friend . . . (Ted Leitner) . . . cards of good wishes by the hundreds . . . rides to physical therapy for days and weeks on end . . . the gifts (quilts, photo albums of my boys while I was in my coma, PJs, etc.), and flowers. Coming home to a home that had been decorated for my family to enjoy Christmas/ And the many hugs.

These are the true signs of Christmas Spirit. My wish for all is that we are all just this lucky at least once in our life. Friends and family love is really all we get to take with us.

Happy Holidays in all of 2001.

Love, Martha & Mark Halda & Our Guys

In early Spring 2002, Ridgeview Church pastor Bill Trok asked if I would be willing to speak to the congregation at a special service the following Sunday. He didn't mention that a harmonica player would accompany me. Thrilled by his request, I accepted. Now, I was nervous. I'd never before spoken to a full congregation that was new to me.

When I walked onto the stage, my heart thumping, I tried to calm myself down. Aaron, Nate, and my family smiled at me. I don't even remember the specifics of what I said, other than sharing the beauty of Heaven and how God cradles us as though we're infants in His arms, and embraces us with beauty and love all the way to Heaven. The next thing I knew, the harmonica player started, and his music transported me back to memories of my youth. On hot summer nights in Carlsbad, my next-door neighbor, David Price, would fill the air with his harmonica. The man on stage was playing a similar type of soothing music. He calmed my shaky nerves.

When I finished my testimony, Pastor Trok began to share that our wonderful harmonica player was a dear friend of his who was dying. This again was another of God's perfect providential plans. While his music was comforting me, my story of Heaven was like rolling out the welcome mat for him.

I rolled this remarkable experience over and over in my mind. I still do it. What this event affirmed to me was one thing: I never knew what miracles, moments of providence or serendipity, or revelations would happen when I shared my story. I just knew that something *would* happen, if only I would keep getting out there.

Chapter 14

Yard by Yard, It's Hard— but Inch by Inch, It's a Cinch

When I finished running track in college, one goal remained: to complete a marathon within five years. Then, I wanted to run another by the time I turned forty. I was a middle distance runner, an eight-hundred-meter girl, and I had always admired runners that had the diligence to step out for a quick fifteen miles, just for fun. What about that is fun?

During track training at North Idaho College in the green hills surrounding the stunning Coeur d' Alene Lake (one of the world's most beautiful, in my opinion), we were expected to log an average of ten miles per day, seventy per week, plus our weight lifting and speed interval work. Due to working, going to class, and studying, I had to make my average runs fifteen miles so I could set aside a few days to open my books. I was never a good student; I had dyslexia, which made spelling and reading tough for me. I had to cram for almost every class.

The fifteen-mile days often started with the off-road trail around Tubb's Hill. Soon enough, my mental block over the distance changed; I noticed that running energized my brain while also firming my body. I also watched the long distance guys with complete admiration. They put in the miles, got excellent grades, partied, and offered the most interesting discussions about all kinds of topics.

One early November day in 1979, I watched the New York Marathon with them in their frat apartment. Wilson Kipsang, a rail thin Kenyan racer, sped to victory in a near world-record time. I had no idea what a large moment was taking place.

My friends did; the apartment erupted. Their excitement caught me by surprise. Then I tried to view the race as they did. I was struck by the determination on Wilson's face, how his toughness and pure focus guided him, and how he was able to kick across the finish line. After twenty-six miles. *Say what?* Wilson raced as if someone were tight on his heels, but his closest pursuer was far back. Still, he pushed across the line.

That was the moment I decided, I wanted that rush. I wanted to know what that felt like. I set my goal to run a marathon in the next five years. However, at the five-year mark in 1984, I found myself married and planning a family, so I reset my target for age forty, or before. Unfortunately, my accident happened when I was forty.

My running and athletic past had served me well during rehab, or so I thought, but I feared any long-distance notions were forever in my past. I was now walking up to a whopping five miles. Deep down, I wanted so much to have more of the old me back. I knew it was going to be a long road, surely more than a wobbly five miles, for me to feel whole. It was going to take Belief.

One night at Bunko (a mindless dice game for ladies), I talked with my girlfriend, Cathey Anderson, who had been participating in 5K and 10K fundraisers, along with a few full and half marathons. I asked Cathey if they allow walking in marathons. "Yes," she said. We agreed she would let me know of any upcoming marathons; perhaps we could walk one together.

That night I was so eager to dream about crossing the finish line that I slipped under the covers feeling again like that teenage tomboy who felt invincible, that she could conquer anything athletically. *I will, I will, I will.* The mantra ran through my head as I lay my head on the pillow.

The very next day, a funny thing happened. A registration form for the Dublin Marathon sat in my P.O. Box, addressed specifically to me! I'd never run a marathon in my life. To top it off, the race was just six months away, in October—the third anniversary to the month of my accident. The invitation came from the American Diabetes Association. Only a few weeks prior, doctors had diagnosed Pops with diabetes and congestive heart failure.

Coincidences? I don't think so. Far beyond it.

As I left the P.O. Box, my eyes filled with tears. I looked straight up to the heavens and said out loud, "Thank you God; count me in." I never thought twice about my ability to actually complete the 26.2-mile race. This was my chance; I would put *all* my belief in God and my ability to persevere. Never mind that I could barely walk five miles when I registered. Participants often fear "hitting the wall" at twenty-mile mark or the sheer pain of those final few miles, but what could be more painful than what I'd gone through?

Sign-ups took place at the same Cardiff By The Sea library where my grandmother took me as a child. Grandma Evie was a kindergarten teacher at the elementary school a block away from the library. When my sister Katie and I had sleepovers at her house, we would visit her classroom to paint, play on the playground out front, and walk over to the library to check out our two to three books for that night's snuggles and reading. The next day was always full of fun at the beaches of Cardiff Campgrounds, playing in the water, and making sand castles. A California girl's idea of perfection. Entering this library was like entering my grandmother's home.

A group of about fifteen were ready to hear more about the invitation they had received. This group quickly dwindled to ten. The girl started off discussing diabetes and how it afflicted so much of the population in the US. She told us about the fundraising, we would each have to raise $3,400 or pay it our self; this would cover all expenses and flights. A few more people left. I was so jacked up and excited; I was committed before I heard any race details. I put my hand up, pulled out my wallet and checkbook. "How do we do this? I'm in; whom do I write a check to? For how much?"

She stopped, astonished. She hadn't even finished her pre-scripted delivery to coax her audience. She looked at me. "Have you done a marathon before?"

"No."

"Don't you want to know more about the fundraising, or the course?"

I started to choke up. *No* . . . I knew God gave this race to me, my dream marathon. I knew I would make it . . . *I would.* These words drummed in my mind, like the famous children's book *The Little Engine That Could*: *I think I can I think I can.* In my case, it was *I know I can, I know I can.*

I'd made the commitment and written the check in the library of my youth with tears running down my face. All the other people looked at me in astonishment. I wanted to get away; my focus was to signup. Also, I didn't want any details on what was afflicting my dad.

The doctors told me soon enough. I had to accept it; my indomitable, deeply loving father was ill. Watching this robust man be affected by two debilitating diseases was probably harder for us than for him. He had coughed often, was walking and moving slower, and the signals were undeniable: He wouldn't be around to give me his gentle guidance much longer.

My dad had always been active in his church. His response to the diagnoses was to attend more. Pops had been a company commander in the Korean War; he had seen it all. He never shared his wartime past with us as kids, but it was understood that Pops avoided hospitals. That is why he hadn't visited me in the hospital until I was lifted from my coma. That is why it was so important for me to share with him first about The Light. I knew how much it took for him to be in that hospital room.

The graceful, elegant way with which Pop dealt with his failing body and situation motivated me even more. He had a REAL strength, a sustained inner strength. *Dammit, if he can have this strength, then so can I.*

I considered my starting point of training: I could walk three to five miles at about a twenty-minute mile. That was it. And I cheated it sometimes. If I felt too slow, I'd take a shortcut across the golf course, hoping no one saw me. Of course, they would have no idea I was cheating, but I would. If they caught me, then I would have to admit it to myself. Ever cheat having just one more cookie?

Then there were my injuries. I had nicknamed my left leg "Driftwood" because it was as useful as a stump, not the stout redwood, but a soft, mushy white pine soaked in the sea. I enjoyed the hills of Pauma Valley the best, but my hips hurt with a stinging sharp pain from my frozen muscles, which would crunch and grind together. They really hurt going up hills, but I turned that into a plea to the Divine: *"Give me feeling, any kind of feeling."* I took glucosamine chondroitin each day, which oiled my joints (a fitting description: I started to think I was the Tin Man from *The Wizard of Oz)*. I sure walked like him, all stiff and upright. I had to stand straight, constantly afraid I would lose my balance and fall, especially when going down those same hills I loved going up. This tilting off balance was caused by my hips being off level about half an inch and from not having nerve feeling in my leg.

Quickly, I realized my upper body would need to help carry my lower body through 26.2 miles. Have you ever wondered why marathoners are ripped all over, even if they're often razor thin? It's because they build their core muscles to provide the strength to push hard during the long race. The most dedicated can feel their upper bodies kick in during uphills, and especially in the final six to eight miles, when the mind begins to wonder why the runner is even on the road.

I knew I would compete in the Dublin Marathon in six months, and raise thousands of dollars along the way. Several family members and friends doubted me. I was so excited to tell my husband. He was an athlete and coach; he'd coached me through some tough times in rehab, so he was going to be elated . . . right?

I'll never forget the look on his face; he looked disgusted. It wasn't quite what I had envisioned. I shared with him how I had written the check, even before the young woman had finished her speech. To top it off, I pledged to either raise the money or pay the fundraising entry minimum myself. I was so thrilled!

The accident had cost more than one million dollars. In an unfriendly way he *was* being logical. He asked me how I thought I would be able to run a marathon when I could barely walk five miles. That stunned me. I knew we didn't have the extra cash, and his fear of me being hurt showed in his words.

"It's not up to me! I know this has been given to me," I cried, frustration in my voice. *Don't tell me I can't do something!*

My husband tilted back his head in disbelief, his mouth dropping open with a huff. "What—" his voice louder than normal "—what do you mean it's been *given* to you?" He had enough of this God thing.

I was crushed; I wanted to slip away from him. What had happened to my guy? The guy who had so eagerly told me he loved me daily since I had returned home? Well, I did not hear that often anymore. I wanted the man with the "can do" attitude, not this hurtful skeptic.

"I'm going to be able to do this, whether you like my God thing or not. I will pay for the fundraising if I need to. But you need to hear me on this: I won't need to." Belief had started! "They gave us a whole guidebook on what our workouts should be and steps for fundraising. I'm gonna be fine, I promise."

I knew this would probably be one of the most significant turning points of my life. I also sensed that I would have to do it without my husband's support.

My soul wept for our love to return.

Dublin resulted in one of the most adventurous, enriching experiences in my life. I competed with more than seven thousand runners. During the race, I drew a lot of my motivation from survivors of various life-threatening diseases, who wore colored jerseys matching their ailments. Whenever I thought, "I can't go on one more step, I need to slow down," I'd see someone in front of me, their jersey "Survivor" announcing they had knocked back cancer, leukemia, cystic fibrosis, diabetes, or some other disease. This helped me to reach down inside myself and grab all the motivation and energy I needed. It helped me squeeze every bit of effort out of my body.

That's not how I felt at the start. We stood way back, in the fundraisers corral, and trudged toward the line, but it was still a rush. The rush I had wanted since Idaho. However, to this California girl it was damp and freezing; I had no idea what to wear for a marathon in a country so many miles away from home. I wasn't sharp enough to think of Googling the weather; it hadn't even crossed my mind. I decided to wear shorts and a tee shirt so I would have the bare minimum clothing over my body. I was used to training in Pauma Valley, in 80- to 100-degree heat. My muscles ached.

Thankfully, my height worked for me. I was able to look over the crowd and watch the frontrunners as they hit the starting line. They bolted forward, zigging and zagging around each other, jockeying for position. I observed, trying to grasp as many tips as I could. I didn't want anyone stepping on my toes or cramping my style.

As we moved forward, I stood with my friend and training partner Mary Brothers. We were trying to hear what the announcer was saying, but the buzz from the crowd was too great. I saw the nervousness on her face and hoped mine didn't show as much. I worried I wasn't in good enough shape. I worried my driftwood leg would go to sleep, that it would give up from being pushed to such a limit. I was petrified I wouldn't make it, and that I would let down all those people, friends, family, and complete strangers that had sponsored me through this endeavor. I was so cold, I needed to move, I was getting claustrophobic, and I thought I would pee my pants right in the middle of this crowd.

The crowd was amazing. I had run 5Ks in college, and those crowds were tight, but this was totally different. So was the pack.

Participants didn't seem to carry that fun, "Let's get her done" atmosphere of 5Ks. Many held their elbows out like sharp wings, marking their bubble of space.

Finally, we moved over the starting line. I broke to the right, a tactic I had watched early from the frontline runners. It freed me from the stifling pack. As Mary and I walked, she chatted with a few other people, but our pace was slowing to the point that it was noticeably slower than our training. Having run 5Ks, I knew this was not something we could maintain and be able to finish. After about seven to eight miles, I told Mary I had to go faster. I needed it; the slower pace was taking its toll on my aching body. I hadn't seen the course and wasn't sure how many hills there were, how high or steep, or when to expect them. I had no idea what to expect.

The Emerald Isle is stunning. This land of green is perfectly named for its pine tree foliage, sweeping grassy meadows, apple green hills, rivers, and rock slate earth. I loved it, and as we moved further into the course, I turned my mind and observant eyes to the landscape. Of course, it was a little easier for me than a Wilson Kipsang: We were at the back of the pack, those "sort of racers." As Bob likes to remind me every time I mention I walked most of it, "Did you finish?"

"Yes . . ."

"Then you did something 99.5 percent of all the people in the world have never done. You started and finished a marathon."

None of that mattered now. We were the fundraisers; we had another reason to finish. I had raised $12,500, one of the largest amounts of any American entrant. All of the money came from one letter chain-mailed to 165 friends—through the post office, not e-mail—and a newspaper article about my attempt. I felt powerful as I walked past the neighborhoods the race wound through. Once I passed the fifteen-mile point, I knew about half of the seven thousand racers had finished. Still, the adorable little pink-cheeked local kids that volunteered were passing out water and oranges. These oranges must cost a fortune to import, a little different than plucking them off the trees on my Pauma Valley training route, where orchards of oranges are abundant. I felt in touch with God . . . the pastors of the many centuries old churches that lined the race, were blessing us as we passed . . . Awesome!

At one point, after I backtracked to get Mary (thus turning my 26.2-mile race into 27 miles; like I needed more), two guys ran up to us, with grins on their faces, wanting to know where we were from. They repeated the question several times before we could understand their thick Irish brogue. We were laughing so hard that it took my focus off my cramping legs. They *loved* my height (I felt like an anomaly), and most of all, that I was a real California girl, hugging them. Back in the day they'd heard the Beach Boys' songs and watched *Baywatch,* so they had a strong perception. It had been their dream to meet a California girl. Here I was, the California girl, fulfilling one of my dreams on their home ground. Pubs lined the race, not a surprise since we were in Ireland and beers and marathoners mix very well. As we passed homes, people stood out on their lawns, or stuck their heads out windows to yell, "Keep going! You're doing great! That's the way, lass."

I tried to stay with Mary and support her, push her along, but in the final four miles, I couldn't handle the slower pace. I looked at Mary said I was sorry, but I had to go. The college athlete had to perform. I started jogging what I assumed was a flat road, but it had a slight incline. I turned the corner and saw an almost twenty-degree incline straight down. It reminded me of the steepest pitch of Middle Grade Road, where my accident took place. My reaction surprised me: *Woo hoo!* I started running, opening my hips to let my legs stretch, a grin crossing my face. Yup . . . I felt like Rocky, because I was now *running* in the marathon. When I reached the bottom, the road turned—and there was the final hill to the finish line. The inner dialogue known to every distance racer kicked in: *Get it girl, give it your all; God's got your back; this is the only time you're doing this, so let's go!*

I ran as fast as I could up that hill. My breathing became rougher; I started wheezing louder. I'm sure I wasn't going fast, but to me, I was bolting. I turned it on, forgot about the broken body beneath my neck, and kicked hard to the finish line. Cheers and applause surrounded me. I looked at the balloon arch and stretched my gait as far as I could, and then slapped my toes on the finish line.

A total of 6,493 runners finished the Dublin Marathon. I was one of them. Just three years before, I was comatose.

Within moments, someone approached me, opening a silver thermal blanket. I dreamt for a moment it was my husband coming to hug and congratulate me. Instead, it was a very kind race volunteer wrapping up my chilled body. My soul screamed in joy. I had finished; no wheelchair for this girl!

I stood around to wait for Mary, beaming as much as I was hurting. As she made her way up that brutal hill, I cheered loudly. To me, there are few things in participatory sports more special than watching runners finish a marathon after you've done it yourself. What a feeling . . . but how I wished I had someone familiar cheering me on.

We returned to our room. Mary closed the bathroom door, gaining the privacy she needed to call her husband and family to share in her victory. She couldn't believe my husband or I hadn't even tried to call each other. In a very weak attempt at deflecting the deep inner hurt that tarnished my achievement, I said, "Oh, with us no news is good news." To me it was unfortunate that I was not celebrating my accomplishment with my husband.

15

Decorating a New Life

What a tumultuous year.

In the winter of 2003, the worst rainstorm since the 1997 El Nino winter hit. It badly damaged our home's roof, and ripped eight-foot sections of our fence from the ground. Those pieces flew down the golf course and landed nearly two hundred feet away, in a neighbor's yard, the eight-foot sections still intact. During the El Nino of 1997, the San Luis Rey River, normally a dry riverbed, busted out of its banks and spilled onto the course. We had given Nate a new bike that Christmas which he had set down on the embankment above the riverbed the night before the storm. A few days later, it was found at the far end of the course, nearly four miles away.

For me, the storm of 2003 was a symbol, omen, and warning, whatever you want to call it. My life was being uprooted. There wasn't going to be peace in our marriage, or home, for what looked to me to be some time.

I spread nine to ten large beach towels on the living room floor to protect against the rain that came through the ceiling. Our insurance company didn't want to cover the five hundred dollars to temporarily cover the roof in plastic. However, after carrying more than $850,000 on my credit for over a year while insurance companies debated how much of my million-dollar hospital bill they would cover, I knew how to deal with them. When I was finished, they paid for a whole new tile roof.

During the process, I learned that if I kept records of whom I talked with, what was said and promised, and listed their names, my cause was helped greatly. However, I hadn't started this because I thought it was smart; I did it because it was the only way I could remember what was happening. I also possessed this sort of inner rage about being treated right, as if my opinion mattered. I still do. In this case, I directed much of my rage into making sure the insurance company took care of our home. The house was a metaphor of our family; I was trying desperately to keep it together.

That wasn't my only source of stress. Money grew tight, and my marriage became far more strained—especially after I returned from the Dublin Marathon. Despite my achievement, which everyone else in my world considered extraordinary, my husband's complaints grew more pronounced. I wanted desperately for our life to return to that of a dream family. I was so crushed. His change since the accident had affected me physically and emotionally. I was the butt of jokes and jabs. We had become roommates; I was now on the level of a college buddy with all the frat house humor that goes along with it. I knew it wasn't initially meant to hurt. I had acquired this style of humor myself. If you can't beat them, join them . . . right? But now it hurt to the core. I wasn't feeling whole. I dreamed of being looked at like before the accident. The Barbie doll Stepford Wife was gone, replaced by this slowly recovering woman.

I sensed trouble, and felt a dire need to contribute to the family finances, and to again become the strong beautiful bride he married. Never mind that I could still turn heads when I showed up at public functions; apparently, that didn't matter anymore.

The one thing I could do, and do well, was decorate and design. I had become a pretty skilled interior decorator. I opened Martha Halda Designs, and *voilà!* One of my first jobs was to decorate the prestigious hotel, The Lodge at Torrey Pines in the exclusive beach town of La Jolla, for the first Christmas since their major remodel. I set up my own little factory in our homes hallway and garage. From there, I created everything to decorate the Lodge's massive lobby, seven banquet rooms, three restaurants, two boutique stores, and the spa.

It didn't feel like work at all. I loved it. I had spent years decorating Bates Nut Farm for the Holidays. I always hosted Thanksgiving and Christmas at my home, in part because I went wild (a thematic, color-coordinated wild!) with decorations. For me, a beautifully decorated Christmas home reflected a well-loved, happy family. As a child, I had helped my mother decorate the Army Navy Academy gymnasium for their winter balls and spring homecoming formals. I learned how to make almost anything from scratch. Stretching further back into my decorating DNA, my dad loved to take his ladies (Mom, Katie, and me) to museums, or shopping sprees at fine stores in the upscale California coastal towns of La Jolla and Laguna Beach. The shopping sprees were for our eyes, not wallets. My parents taught me to notice and appreciate quality and beauty in décor (even on a dime). I can still hear my mother's admonition: "It needs to match." Didn't matter what it was; make sure it matches. I'm still that way. It drives my sons crazy.

My dad really looked out for my creative side, which he recognized early on. One time when I was maybe eight, he signed me up for art lessons in San Clemente, about 25 miles up the coast. While my mom would take the other kids to the beach, my brother would dive for abalone, and I would ride to my art lessons. I always loved color, from the turquoise of the ocean, the reds and pinks of carnations that grew next door, to the blue sky that makes Southern California the place to be—especially in winter. I think of the colors I saw in Heaven and how our most brilliant earthen colors are rather only muddy versions.

I was so lucky to have landed The Lodge and I knew it, thanking God daily. To add to my good fortune, the owners wanted The Lodge dressed in a natural Williamsburg Christmas, designed and guided by natural and organic elements. They asked me to fill the trees with fresh fruit, oranges, apples, lemon and Magnolia blossoms. The Garlands and wreaths had Pineapples and lemons. It was no mistake to me that my first job would glorify God. After all, it was Christmas, and my life's history had prepared me; to me it was just another display of how my life was already planned. Providence had once again shown up in my life.

Along with my contract came quite a perk—three nights at the Lodge. These rooms usually ran $400 to $1,000 per night. What a great place for my husband and I to spend some badly needed time together, to get our marriage back on track! However, he determined that he needed to stay focused on work. We filled his Suburban with all the crates of the ornaments I had made and selected for each of the trees. I talked him into helping me deliver them, hoping he would see how awesome the rooms were and decide to stay a night or two with me . . . but that didn't happen. I had already made plans for the boys to stay at their grandmother's house. The bellboys unpacked the goods and loaded them into my staging room. No look at the room, no snuggle, no kiss. He drove off.

One of the bellboys, maybe twenty-five years old, made a comment that will forever echo in my consciousness. I wasn't meant to hear it as the Suburban drove off; he said, "Man, if I had her here, I sure wouldn't be driving off; what a dude." His remark forced me to realize that we were at the last straw. I thought I was hiding it well, but he must have seen a look of longing on my face.

I went to my room and called my sister Katie, crying and begging her to stay and enjoy the room with me. Like the loving, caring big sister she is, she immediately drove down, we enjoyed wine and a wonderful dinner, and strolled the coastal property that sits right on the golf course, above the Pacific.

The next day, my girls from Valley Center came out to serve as my decorating crew. I had to face them as their leader. As much as I wanted to climb into a hole and weep, I couldn't; now was the time for strength. Funny, I always have that strength. I can't figure where it comes from, but I have it when I need it. Maybe those years as the youngest kid with three older brothers prepared me to have the strength when I needed it. This time, however, I girded myself from witnessing a moment from my life preview in Heaven playing out on earth. I had been shown the end of my marriage. Now, I just had to accept it. But I wasn't willing yet.

A few months later, in May 2004, Palomar Hospital contacted me to ask if I would be willing to assist them in fundraising. They knew what my answer would be; I would do anything to help Palomar Hospital. Except end up in their intensive care unit again!

I was willing to fundraise in any way possible. I had some experience, fundraising for the Valley Center School PTA for 12 years as my boys grew up. I was the Little League snack bar organizer, the room mom, and the Pop Warner Football team mom. Each of these posts required fundraising and motivational skills. Most importantly, I had fundraised for the Dublin Marathon, choosing my words correctly for the letter I wrote, and choosing my words correctly during the interview for the article that was written. Yet, the Palomar Hospital request really made me feel of value. I was going to help give back to the hospital that had saved my life. Well, I always said (from day one) Dr. Cloyd with the grace of God saved my life. Now I even joked to my friends that there are few men I know who walk on water, and Dr. Cloyd is one of them. Again, I was to be up front of the crowd. Again, I would need to choose my words carefully.

Two months later, I spoke at The Volunteer Round Up, which featured a dinner held on the magnificent De Jong property in Valley Center. It was one of the loveliest cocktail parties I've ever attended. I wandered through the crowd, looking for a familiar face. I wished I had someone special by my side, someone that was good at this stuff, someone like my husband. He had not wanted to come. People chatted with me without having any idea who I was. That's the way it is at a cocktail party. I kept moving, hoping no one would notice I was not attended by a date; this was surely not a pickup crowd! I enjoyed the early twentieth-century adobe home, the lush, perfectly manicured grounds, and the property's willow trees which looked like something from a movie.

For dinner, chicken had been grilled on open metal tub style BBQs, creating a real Western round-up feel, right down to the metal plates we used. My table sat up front on the grass near the gazebo, the de facto anchor for the stage. I chatted with my group.

Towards the end of dinner, a gentleman asked why I was there and who had invited me.

Before I could answer, the emcee started her introductions and I began to get nervous. *I don't want to mess this up; I don't know what I should say, so I'm going to just give it over to God.* When I was introduced, my dinner accomplice smiled and said, "Well played." Raising his eyebrows and smiling, he nodded, as if to suggest, *now go get them!*

I walked up, smiled, and looked at the crowd in this wonderland setting, which sort of reminded me of the mist-filled entrance to Pirates of the Caribbean at Disneyland. I certainly felt like I was at Disneyland; having a home and property this spectacular was quite a fantasy.

My eyes glided from left to right, scanning the crowd. I tried to make contact with each of the roughly five hundred guests. I opened my mouth and had no idea what words came out, but they seemed to flow nicely. Later, one of the attendees recapped for me: I described the hills of Pauma Valley and Valley Center. I talked about how minutes made a difference in my life, how blessed we were to have the fantastically gifted doctors at Palomar, and how we needed to get them what they lacked. Then I told my story. Afterwards, I took a page from Hillary Clinton's playbook to stress the need to improve Palomar's trauma unit, saying, "As a community, we need to act as a village." I then asked everyone to pull out their wallets and open their checkbooks. They smiled, people began to clap, and I noticed checkbooks out and pens scribbling. The event was a big success.

Besides the money, I noticed something else in the candlelight: the sparkling tears of guests. *Wow!* I felt so much at peace, whole and part of a community. I wanted to share my story even more; I started to understand why God had me make that promise: *If I get to go back, I promise I will tell. I will tell of your greatness, I will tell of your Love.*

Sometimes Love manifests in the form of a donation to a good cause. The hospital knew they had me hook, line, and sinker. I would speak for them, I would ask for nothing, and I would do it whenever. Plus, I noticed people like hearing my story!

In August, I shot a TV commercial for the hospital, addressing the need for improved trauma units and to promote a special bond measure, set to appear on the November ballot. The $496 million bond measure, Proposition BB, would fund major hospital renovations in North San Diego County. On the hot summer day, the commercial producer brought two small actors to portray my kids. They definitely had the best part, jumping and frolicking in our pool while we filmed. I'm not an actress, so it took hours to get about ten minutes of commercial. My commercial ran at least fifteen times per day on network affiliates in San Diego and neighboring Riverside counties. The public service announcement made quite an impact: The bond measure, the largest ever in San Diego County, passed, and funded the new state of the art hospital.

However, it also impacted our home, causing yet another emotional challenge. My spouse did not like the idea of me being on TV, which he considered his turf. He didn't seem to mind so much about the commercial running in San Diego County, but when he found it also was running in Riverside, he grew furious. "You're really going to have this air everywhere, are you?" *Like I had a say!*

"Where did you see it in Riverside?" I asked excitedly. All I wanted to know was the channel. Easy enough, right?

He was not so excited. In fact, he didn't want me to know where he saw it, much less the channel! That was odd, even for him. I couldn't wrap my head around his anger. It felt insane to me for anyone to object to my purposeful act to help the hospital, something that would help so many people.

People started to identify me as a TV spokesperson, as that lady in the commercial. I viewed the commercial exactly for what it was—a very grateful woman giving back to the hospital that saved her life.

No doubt remained any longer; our marriage was a train wreck at the crashing point.

Giving Back—

Starting Over

In March 2004, a few days after my forty-fifth birthday and four and a half years after my accident, I filed for divorce. In a never-ending series of final straws, the culmination came on the night of my birthday. After returning home from our family night out, I saw the pain in my boy's eyes as they watched me cry. It was time. I had to finally accept what God had shown me during the review, that while my husband and I might be good people separately, we could not continue together.

The next morning, I called my dad, and let him know what I needed to do. He asked me to come by the house. We had a long talk. Divorce was not part of our family, and certainly not taken lightly; we all tried to live the "until death do us part" portion of the marriage vow. "How do you feel?" Dad asked. "What do you think God's position on this would be?"

This was a new line of communication between my dad and me. Our family didn't talk to each other about religious or political viewpoints. However, my dad realized I now thought about things in a spiritual way. I told him I'd already visited with Pastor Sale on this subject. Pastor Sale had prayed intently over me in the hospital, and had given me laying on of hands healing for many consecutive days when I was battling to survive the accident. He desperately pleaded as my emissary to God to heal me.

I met with Pastor Sale, told him how things were going with our marriage, and of my fear that divorce was not biblical. He asked me many questions before reaching across the desk and gripping both my hands. "Let's pray," he said, reaching out as my emissary once again.

Afterwards, he looked straight at me. His next comment caught me by surprise. "I will show you at least ten different ways and passages in which your covenant with your husband has been broken," he said, "and how it will be sound and biblical with God if you choose to go forward in divorce. "

My dad was relieved; he knew this was not a spur-of-the-moment decision. I shared how I had pleaded for counseling with my husband, but to no avail. Pops simply got up, went to the kitchen, and returned with a check for $3,000. With a bittersweet smile, he said, "it's probably not enough, but this should get a lawyer, and get the ball rolling. It's time for the ball to be in your court."

I had spent years training Aaron and Nate to be gentlemen, and how to treat a lady. It was due to emotional neglect and issues I couldn't then forgive (forgiveness is crucial for love) that I decided to end our pain. To me, it was far more important to show my boys that some things just aren't meant for a family to endure. "You choose your life, and how your treat a person is the reflection of your inner choices," I told them. "Truthfulness is the most important thing in life."

I meant it; it came from the person I'd become since the accident. I believed, and still believe, that truthfulness is the most important aspect of love, and love is the essence of our souls. You can't truly love anything or anyone without being truthful about everything. Truth causes you to be unguarded, unashamed, and to unveil yourself completely. It is the height of openness, transparency and vulnerability, and we all know what happens when those three dynamics combine. Relationships flourish. When you are in Heaven, your soul is completely unveiled—God sees and knows everything about us. As I see it, he created us and designed our full life in a master plan, a master blueprint for our lives. You see this in Eastern spiritual teachings, too, in what is called in India the Akashic Records—a "noting" of everything good and bad we've done, and how they measure up to our master plans. There's no covering up or hiding in Heaven, just as there shouldn't be on earth. I felt all God wanted from me was to live in my authentic self.

Now I had to face my own music: My life was not turning out as the perfect dream I wished for as a little girl. I was very sad, but still certain I would continue to laugh, cry, love, and unreservedly share all of the good, the bad, and myself. I also knew it would be years before I would feel comfortable enough to bring myself fully forth in another relationship.

Besides the hurt of losing something into which I'd poured my life, I realized that, after twenty-one years of marriage, most of it as a stay-at-home mom, I had nothing to offer an employer. Then I remembered something: I had accomplished a lot. Every morning, I repeated to myself, *Honey, if you can teach yourself to walk again, you can do anything! Now pull yourself up by the bootstraps and get your chin up.* I chuckled sometimes when I said this, because, as a Southern California beach girl, I wore sandals. I didn't even own a pair of boots!

I knew I needed to be strong, to restore my inner and outer confidence. I needed to find the guts of that athlete who always kicked the final one hundred meters to the finish line. Still, it was awkward, and challenging. We sat next to each other on the couch when I brought up my feeling that we needed to divorce. My husband laughed. "You're never gonna divorce me. You don't have the guts."

"Funny, I filed the day after my birthday," I said. "I told the lawyer I wanted it done in the shortest time allowable. He says it takes six months. The way I see it, we both will be giving up a lot, but let's just get it done."

We lived in the house together while figuring out the next step. It was odd, almost eerie. We actually got along better, but that may have been because we weren't at odds anymore; we had given up "being together." I felt treated with more respect and kindness than I had been in a very long time. When asked if we could somehow bypass the divorce and try to work it out, my simple reply was, "All it will take is honesty and an apology."

Apparently, that was too much to ask.

Every day, I made a new commitment to myself, holding my little personal track meet. If I won for the day, then I got a medal (so to speak). It reminded me of when my boys were little. They had a chart on the refrigerator. If they completed the chore on the chart, they got a gold star. My goal was to earn all gold stars. I made little deals with myself, which at the time did not feel so little: *If you don't cry today, Martha, then treat yourself to a Starbucks, or go enjoy the peace of the driving range with a bucket of golf balls.*

I re-entered the workforce as a teller at the local bank. I was forced to get a grip on my ravaged emotions daily; folks came in and wanted to know more about the demise of my marriage. Believe me, when snoops greet you and the face of the Grinch lies beneath their pasted-on smiles, you learn the meaning of holding a stiff upper lip. Because of my new viewpoint, I was not afraid or overly stressed. I knew that I would make it, that each challenge was a learning phase for me. I knew that God's plan was already set, and I would be fine.

Thankfully, all the women at the bank were wonderful, including Wendy, my "cubby buddy" (we shared the same teller stall), and my longtime friend Carolyn Zajda. I had babysat Carolyn's kids after school years before I started at the bank. More than once, Carolyn met me in the lounge room and let me unload or cry after a client had felt the need to know more of my personal life, and ask those unintended, yet hurtful, questions. I focused on the thought that every step, experience, encounter, and circumstance happens to prepare us for the next step to come.

I only had one question: Would I be able to take that next step?

I also encountered people outside the bank, church ladies in particular, who didn't like my comments about seeing an Angel or much else about my time in Heaven. Ironic, isn't it? We talk about Heaven in many different religions, in churches throughout the world, as the grand afterlife, the reward of Christianity. Yet, some ladies found special exception in the fact that I didn't see family members or friends when I passed over. In their view, if I was good and went to Heaven, I should have seen family or friends. Everyone seemed to be an expert . . . most certainly, they added, if I was a good Christian woman, I wouldn't be getting a divorce.

Ouch . . . that hurt. I already had enough difficulty with this situation.

I tried to prove them wrong, that I was a good Christian woman, so I volunteered at the church bookstore. Again a few shoppers asked, in different ways, "What scripture have you found that qualifies your thoughts that you passed over?" Why did these churchgoers, my sisters in Christ, seem to find it the hardest to believe that someone could have a near-death experience, a taste of eternity? *Hey, ladies, I already know; I experienced it. I don't need to find it in writing. I'm too busy enjoying life, I don't want to be judging people. Besides, doesn't that same Bible say it's not for us to judge?*

Some people can't accept what they haven't seen, touched, or felt for themselves. (I totally get this. Until passing over, I sure as heck didn't believe in Angels, or the Trinity [Father-Son-Holy Spirit to Christians; Om-Tat-Sat to Hindus.])

I had the faith that comes from knowing what I experienced was 100 percent real. Faith can go a long way, but first I needed to get out of my own way. I needed to neutralize my own mighty ego.

For me, the essence of spirit is sharing, caring, love, and the unity of all things. I mean *all* things: I saw, while in Heaven, that everything is energy. I had watched as particles throughout a meadow came together and re-formed into a waterfall. Everything existed to bring love, healing, and pleasure. Which led me to three questions that, I knew, would be guideposts for my future dealings with others:

How was I to deny that?

How was I supposed to convey or share this without alienating people?

How was I supposed to fit into a box of a certain mind-set of one church?

My solution? I mixed it up. I went to one church on Sundays, I'd take Nate to youth group at another Church, and I attended a Bible study with women from all sorts of churches. I couldn't accept one church that thought I had to sing this way, dress that way, or conduct my Bible study in their prescribed manner. I've always had trouble being told what to do. I played a sort of hop-scotch game, back and forth, between churches.

Soon, it began to work for me.

Thankfully, I felt safe within my family, because they didn't view me differently at all. Nor did we talk about my time in Heaven much. It may have changed their views of life indirectly, but that was their personal thing. I did know my children and siblings had acquired a beauty inside their souls, knowing that God is there for each of us, and there is no reason to fear death. I shared that almost daily.

There was one person I particularly wanted to know this: my dad. Pops's health was getting worse. He was on his way out after his long, wonderful life on Earth. I felt an almost urgent need; I wanted him to know where he and his soul were going next.

Through all of this, I strove to understand how and why virtually all religions claim that their path is the only "right" path, the only road that leads to Heaven. I had seen something completely different; the loving embrace of God. I contend that if people will open their hearts and minds to another's way, they will see the commonality in our beliefs, customs, and lifestyles. Plus, there are no labels or "road signs" with religious denominations painted on them in Heaven.

A few of my neighborhood country club ladies also acted differently toward me. Their hang-up didn't concern my talk about Angels, Heaven, or passing over. They now gave me funny looks because I was the divorcée down the street, the young blonde woman who was suddenly *available*. I felt that, in their own minds, they worried I would somehow swoop in on their husbands. *Hey girls, I'm still the same person! I didn't want your dude before, so why would I want him now?* As for getting together with a man because of his money? Not my style. And certainly not when he's wearing a ring! I still pick the guy that has an interesting mind before I pick the guy with money. (Good lord; sometimes I wish I could fix this pattern.)

It's odd. When a couple divorces, their friends feel they need to choose which partner deserves their continued friendship. Maybe it's easier for them, but believe me, it's not easier for the one not being chosen. During these situations, which filled me with hurt and anger, I remembered a lesson from eternity: I never want to go through a life review in which I experienced the negative feelings I passed onto others. That lesson was tested, more than once.

I had to figure out what kind of friends I wanted. I had my Bunko group of nearly ten years; they were my rock. These Ya Yas, as we called ourselves (after Rebecca Wells' great book, *Divine Secrets of the Ya-Ya Sisterhood)*, were twelve women that served as friends, parents, counselors, and cheerleaders.

I wanted to know why I thought something, why I felt something, and why people treated each other the way they did. It was odd and driving me a little nutty. But for now, I needed to stop my wandering thinking and focus, and find a job that would pay a mortgage. I thought of something else I'd heard before. Often when we lose hope and think it's the end, God smiles from above and says, "Relax, it's just a bend, not the end!"

Little did I know that the real estate class I had taken in 2001 would lead to my new direction. I couldn't support myself on my part-time bank teller job, so I fell back on my distant past as a property appraiser in Idaho, plus the real estate class. I decided to cram for a real estate license. I studied eighteen hours a day for three straight days, and I passed the test. I wasn't surprised; I knew I would pass. I had the same confidence as when I played tennis; there wasn't an opponent that frightened me. The way I saw it was that, even if I lose, I still win, because I'm out there doing it. It didn't matter to me if the "it" was tennis, running, baking, gardening, or job hunting. I needed to take this mind-set and get going. My next challenge was to get hired.

Through his years of running a mortgage company, my soon-to-be ex-husband enjoyed contacts with many of San Diego County's larger homebuilders. He gave me their information. I met with Jeff, the Director of Sales for Barrett American . . . and was hired!

Immediately, I set my goal: to become their number one sales person. I was to be their agent on wheels. Once it was discovered I was divorcing his friend, I was swapped out from one location track to the next almost weekly. However, this served to my advantage. This gave me more knowledge in a shorter amount of time; you can't be idle when learning a new floor plan, location, and township constantly. I greeted buyers for homes in Del Mar that started from $2.7 million, then off to Temecula, where the floor plans were almost identical but the prices far more affordable: $500,000 to $700,000. I enjoyed these lovely, massive, stunningly appointed homes on golf courses or with ocean views. I also enjoyed meeting my prospective buyers . . . but something seemed to be missing. The something wasn't missing from me alone; it also seemed to be missing from a lot of the buyers. My world was all about things and positions, and I wasn't finding pleasure in the pretense that having more makes you somehow better or happier. I yearned for more.

Chapter 17

Looking for Romance and a Good Life

Over the next several years, my life drastically changed. Again it occurred to me these hardships were actually shown to me during my life review/preview.

The destiny shown to me indicated that I would divorce, part of my trade to come back to mother my sons. Knowing this and acknowledging it ahead of time made the whole process far less painful. I was also shown that possessions were not the true gold that really mattered; I would appreciate this even more a few years later. Most importantly, I was reminded that love is the most important gift. When people didn't accept me any longer, I grew to be at peace and tried to remain loving anyway. This made the transitions in my life much easier.

I had a few things I remembered crisply; I knew they were planned, but there was so much more I didn't know on the fore-front. Yet, it was imbedded in my soul; I experienced that déjà vu feeling often, but then it would occur to me that what I saw or felt didn't match any previous experience in my life on Earth. I was baffled, but I figured this was the way God wanted it. He had plans for my life, they were already orchestrated, and he was the conductor. I could and would survive.

The Fragrance of Angels

These odd circumstances still happen. I don't remember all the details of what I saw and was shown—that is, until something happens. But when the time arrives, it all comes rushing back. I experience *déjà vu*.

I developed my own calming meditative practice, equal parts prayer and meditation, to keep the feeling of loss minimal after my divorce. When driving out of Pauma Valley, in the early morning heading east into sunrise, I'd drive through the mist and watch the sunshine bolt down through the clouds to the valley floor, and I looked up at the rays as if they were God shining down on earth. *Good morning, God.* I started this with Nate on the way to school, when we would smile and happily greet God in the morning. Nate was good humored about this, never getting upset or thinking his mom was whacked, a crazy church lady, or some nutty extreme Bible thumper. I was just Mom to him, and he liked God well enough, so why not say good morning to Him?

We had another recurring prayer. When we heard a fire engine or ambulance siren, we would say a prayer for the EMTs working inside the vehicle, to give them strength to do their job and the calmness and knowledge to take care of their sick or injured passenger. Please bring them home safely at the end of the day. We also prayed for the person in need, asking that God would give them peace. At first I said these out loud, but soon we did so silently. However, the good morning to God was said out loud, usually followed by cranking up the music. I don't know about Nate, but I sure loved my morning drives, and we both loved our music.

Later, when Nate was in high school and college, he would start my day by setting up his guitar and amp in the living room; the vaulted ceiling and tile floors made for awesome acoustics, so he would let it rip. I would get my own serenade to start the day, and he knew what I liked: Carlos Santana, at mega decibels.

Now that my marriage was over and my latest source of great stress was of job stability, or rather, lack of it. I continued to find it difficult to understand the comments people made directly to me; many were astonishing, and not in a positive way.

Some people think near-death experiences are a psychological disorder probably caused be the lack of oxygen, or trauma to the brain. I actually had people say to me, "You were surely out of your mind from the drugs or pain." The most memorable comments seemed to come whenever I talked about being with an Angel. The response would usually be something like, "It wasn't real; it was just a figment of your imagination." This one would make me smile or laugh; it still does. *No one will ever get me to believe that Angels are imaginary.* Why would anyone in their right mind choose to say they saw an Angel if they hadn't? Why would anyone knowingly welcome ridicule? I don't get it. Science defines my view of seeing an Angel as forms of dissociation, the separation of thoughts or experiences from the normal stream of consciousness. Examples include daydreaming, psychogenic amnesia, reactions to some drugs, and multiple personalities.

I didn't have psycho anything. If I had not made a promise to "the Big Man," I sure wouldn't be coming out with my experience or this book. Since I did make God this promise, I'm certainly going to fulfill it. You don't knowingly "choose" to go against the most loving, powerful, and divine presence . . . now that would be crazy!

Aaron had graduated from high school two years before, in 2003. He had a steady girlfriend Amy (whom he would marry in July 2012), so he was not around much. I left every day at 7 a.m. to sell homes, and returned at 7:30 every night. To top it off (or bottom it down), I didn't have weekends off. Nate, who was now driving, was affected most, since he only knew me as a stay-at-home mother. Thankfully, he was active in several youth groups. They became his surrogate family. I grew jealous of them all; I just wanted to experience the life I used to have.

My home and family nest shrank. My boys were becoming the independent, strong men I had wanted them to grow into. I was still selling homes and doing a fine job, but it wasn't enough.

At Barrett American, my employer, I shared my story with a few chosen girls. They found out in 2005 during a synergy team meeting, part of a sales training seminar, when we were given the task of making a vision board of our dreams. I split my board into three sections: present and future travel; the future of my sons; and my retirement. In this final column, I drew a book end and wrote a title: *A Taste of Eternity.* I stood up in front of the group to explain my board. During my explanation of the third column, I stared at their shocked faces. I also told them about learning to walk and talk again; they had seen for themselves how much I struggled with computer skills that once were second nature. I was lucky enough to have a few patient women help me with the basics, but at first, it felt like Aztec to me.

One day when still working with Barrett American, I spoke with Sherryln, my biggest ally. I asked her what she wanted from me that day, since she was going to be off-site. "I want a down deposit," she said. (This was not the easiest request to fulfill; a deposit was $50,000.) To her surprise and mine, when she returned at 4 p.m., I presented her not with just one but two checks.

Meanwhile, another very deep sadness came calling: My Daddy's time in this world was ending. When I visited with him, Pops always asked if I would share my experience of Heaven. He again encouraged me to write this book; after all, I'd known the title since waking from my coma. As the one-time reference librarian and book buyer at Carlsbad City Library, he loved everything to do with books and the minds that created them. I never saw myself as someone who could write a book, but he certainly did. Dad also reminded me I was beautiful, strong, and full of love, and I needed to find someone to love, that someone special to share my life with. My parents had only ever been married to each other, so this is what he knew, a bond between two people, an understanding of the other person, their ups and their downs. A coupling where each person is the other half of a whole—that's what Pops wanted for me.

Dad still found his way to Sunday service, often on days I'd come visit. We liked it best when it was just the two of us. If my mom or siblings were there, he didn't feel comfortable digging deeply into conversation; he was a one-on-one communicator. We'd sit in the back living room, often eating BLT sandwiches or tomato soup (these will forever be comfort food to me). It was almost like a child's story time. Pops would hunker down in his comfortable chair with a blanket resting over his knees, look at me, and ask, "What can you tell me today?" He loved to hear about the Angels singing, which triggered a memory: how I got kicked out of the church choir in third grade because the director could not find a way to disguise my off-key voice. We laughed hard about that. "What would they do in this case in Heaven?" I asked Dad rhetorically. "I mean, can you kick out an Angel?" Probably not, I guessed; in the perfection of the Divine, all Angels have perfect pitch, right?

Pops was beginning to lose his breath and the fight; the diabetes was weakening his heart. Some days, we would just sit and I would hold his hand.

After months of being traded out from track home project to track home project, I followed one of my managers who had changed positions to another builder. One day, she called me to represent another location. Linda treated me like I was a valued sales person, one in which she saw talent. I appreciated her belief in me and followed her to this new builder thankfully. I focused on the new community of homes, growing daily in my abilities and creative ideas for marketing the site. My confidence became much stronger, I was adaptable if not comfortable with the computer once again, and I was very skillful and lighthearted conversing with the prospective buyers. I could describe each product, appliance, or upgrade offered, all while smiling and qualifying my possible buyer. It felt good. I realized my mind was fully functioning again. (Woo, that was a welcome relief!) Soon, I became the manager for this track. This community was all on me; I was to run the whole show. One couple came in and their taste was higher than this neighborhood, and they had friends who were my neighbors in Pauma Valley. They wanted a home similar to what we enjoyed in the country club, but without the same price point. My mission that day was to show them all of the qualities we offered; when we were done, they handed me a check and signed a contract. When that happened, I knew I was good at whatever I put my mind to.

Thankfully I was now located in Escondido, much closer to home. I could see Nate's water polo games or whatever else he was involved with. So I hoped. Nope . . . Nate was into his own gig, and into that challenging teenage mind-set for a parent that goes like this: *Mom, I don't really need you.* He didn't need me, but I certainly needed him.

I was feeling the need for love. I understood instinctively that love is not just for people. Every living being on earth is made up of essentially the same energy, particles, and spirit matter. Look into the eyes of any creature, your pet dog or cat, or any wild animal; I did it often with my dogs, Stormy and Bo. Take a detailed account of a mother-infant relationship and every friendship, and feel the need and desire for love. Love knows no boundaries. However, I wanted to see this and feel it, not just know and understand it.

I felt lost. I started feeling the urge to date, but I'd totally forgotten how after twenty-one years off the market! The idea of dating was so strange. For one thing, I had no feeling of self worth, and I mentally exaggerated the grotesqueness of my scars. I was petrified of ever having to show them to a possible new man. At work, I felt strong and smart, because I knew my product . . . but a date? I found myself suddenly having to ad-lib, talk about myself, and go where the conversation flowed. I wasn't sure I would ever be entertaining enough for the man to ask me on a second date. When you're married, you don't have to share who you are. Your partner already knows. Or, they should, right?

I worried how would I explain how I sometimes don't remember names, moments, or even places. How would I share that I might seem distant to my date when I see something beautiful, or freak out in a car if I'm not the one driving? I didn't have to explain these challenges to my spouse; he already knew the what, when, where, and why. I actually hoped it would be like before I was married, when men rarely asked me out, due to my height of six-foot-one.

For the next five years, I dated three men. Each gave me something I had been missing for the past twenty years.

I met Rick at the Oceanside beach amphitheater (now the Junior Seau Amphitheatre, named after a Hall of Fame American football player, who grew up in Oceanside). Rick was the ex-brother-in-law of a couple I had known for the last thirty years. We were introduced, and he spent the rest of the concert trying to find a way to get my number. He succeeded. What fun we had, he was always laughing and enjoying the moment! He made me feel beautiful, often telling me this. He told me my thick, chest-to-navel scar was nothing to worry about. "It's barely noticeable," he said . . . what a salesman! However, soon I was ready to buy it. I felt like a puppy, ready to eat out of his hand if he just kept telling me this. I hadn't heard that I was beautiful for years. Comfortable as our friendship was, I didn't go into any depth of what I experienced in Heaven with him. I don't know why; maybe it was because I figured out quickly he would always be a lifelong friend, not a life partner. We dated for six or seven months.

My next sweetheart was Russell. I caught up with him out dancing one evening when a friend's band was playing at a restaurant in my hometown of Carlsbad. I had always adored him and found him to be a mystery, since he was shy . . . until you got to know him. We loved the ocean and spent time walking the beaches, talking. Russell was and is sweet beyond comparison. We had known each other for most of our lives; I loved his surfer-boy appeal for what it was. He was about five-foot-eight, a stunning Asian surfer boy, with silky, long brown hair to his shoulders, next to my six feet—well, we made quite the pair. He was just right. The only problem was, he started trying to change his casual attire and personality to please me, to make me happy. After a short three to four months, I told him I had to break it off because I felt I would only break his heart. I loved him the way he was and didn't want to damage his sweet soul by allowing him to change for me. I didn't feel I was worthy. A sweeter man I have never known.

Months later, at a concert at the Pala Casino near my home, I spotted Earl. He combined the manners and etiquette my parents had instilled in me. He spoiled me like a beautiful queen he could lavish, dress up, and take out for lovely evenings at wonderful restaurants in the Dana Point or Newport Beach areas. Earl also loved R&B and soul music, which made him a rarity: a man that liked music and to dance as much as I did. As an added bonus, he was six-foot-four, Thursdays off, and loved to golf. So did I. We spent many Thursdays on the golf courses of Laguna Beach and Costa Mesa. He didn't have any hang-ups about women not being as good as men; as long as I wanted to play, he was willing to take me. Some of my coworkers would joke that I should write a different kind of book, called *Thursdays Off*. Little did they know I already had a book in mind. I dated Earl for three years on and off; it lasted that long because we only saw each other once every other week. I didn't tell Earl much about my Angel, but I did share portions of my experience and he loved every description I shared. I guess it was me; I was still guarded, not wanting to be judged or have them think I was mentally off. One of the reasons I loved each of them is that they had responded to me in a positive way, filling me with loving attention after I'd craved it for years.

Did you notice this correlation between men, music, and me? There was more to come.

On the work front, the economy and real estate industry headed south big-time, in what would become a global recession—and, in some cases, a depression. I changed industries and started selling timeshares before moving into contracts and quality assurance for one of California's largest time-share companies. I had sold new homes because I felt a family's love was based in the home . . . what better thing to sell than homes?

Then I remembered that all you get to take with you are your memories (no U-Hauls in Heaven). Where do you make the most, strongest, and best memories? On vacation! This was where my memories with my boys were the strongest, on those vacations I could no longer afford. With timeshare, I could help people and families find a way to build those valuable memories in an affordable way. I still work in the industry for this reason. However, there is a shadow side to timeshare, a greedy thirst for money among some of the salespeople—just as there is in many professions. I lost myself briefly in a more hedonistic lifestyle of money, money, money, and having fun. While my job continued to bolster my confidence, I struggled to pay the hefty mortgage of our family home. Life became a daily task of keeping my head above water, keeping my house, and paying for college and cars for my boys.

Mainly, I missed my own heart; why was I lonely, what was missing, why wasn't I able to really love anyone? I couldn't understand. Why did God give me a choice to return to such a difficult life? Why didn't he let me stay in Heaven, when this was my preference? I had never asked myself these questions before, even when learning to walk and talk again.

I found myself asking these questions regularly.

Chapter *18*

Life Changes of Love

By 2010, I felt exhausted. No matter how I tried to bolster myself, I was just tired. Also, for some strange reason, my abdomen kept getting larger; so much so that I had to keep buying pants the next size up. I was becoming reclusive, not wanting to do anything but work and then go home and sleep. If you know me, you know that is the opposite of my normal demeanor; I love being with and around people.

One night in April, a longtime friend, known to many as JJ, called and asked me to join him with a group of hometown high school friends. I knew I needed to get out, so I agreed to travel with him and my friend Jaimee up the coast to Dana Point, to see a friend's band play at Hennessy's, a local restaurant and bar. A bunch of high school friends would be there, he said. I dressed, put on my smile, and away we went.

When we arrived, I saw nearly twenty Carlsbad buddies. While sitting with a girlfriend, Sheila, we chatted about our life changes, and how she had just recently filed for divorce. Since I'd been divorced for five years, I was able to share some advice on coping with sadness, anger, and sense of loss. Then I looked over the crowd while enjoying the band, whose bass player/back-up singer, Willy, I'd known since kindergarten. As I did, I watched a handsome man with a full head of hair, chiseled jawline, and wonderfully fit body glide past the window outside. He caught my attention. *Finally . . . now that's a guy I'd like to meet.*

Sheila waved at him. I leaned in and asked, "Who is that?"

"Oh, that's Bob."

"Bob who?"

"You know him, Martha. Bob Yehling."

I tried to remember while being blasted by the music from my friend's band, which always played a little loudly. *Hmmm, I think I've heard that name before, but still . . .* "No Sheila, really I don't know anyone named Bob, not one that looks like that," I said.

She looked at me, now as confused by my lack of recognition as I was about the man's identity. "Of course you know who he is—Robert Yehling."

"Oh . . . well yeah I know Robert Yehling." I looked again, as he walked through the door. This wasn't the Robert I remembered! "He changed his name to Bob after high school," she continued. I thought, while looking him up and down, *a lot more than his name has changed.*

I wasn't listening anymore. I was watching. He glided into the bar, walking with determination toward us. Unlike me, he recognized everyone in the room, although he hadn't seen any of us besides Sheila and another childhood friend, Teresa, since high school. *Good God,* my mind chastised me, *he's coming right to us. Did he see my eyes feast on his chest? Did he notice me checking him out through the window?*

Bob sat down between Sheila and I. They'd gone out to lunch a few times, not really dating, but more to rekindle the close friendship they'd had in junior high and high school.

It was time for this girl to act. I wanted to talk with him to draw his attention away from Sheila. I related the story of how years earlier Kris called him my "boyfriend," which drew a hearty laugh from both of us. I thanked him for his generous and kind words about me, in his letter to the editor response way back in May of 2000. It was now 2010; I wasn't sure he would remember it or me.

Bob then said something that really warmed my heart. "I dreamed more than once in high school of you being my girlfriend," he said. "My buddies and I would sit by the door in creative writing class, and watch the morning parade—you and a few other girls would walk by with your long legs in your short shorts. But you were out of my league; plus, I was quite a bit shorter than I am now."

Fair enough!

We talked about all sorts of things: the music, the beauty of Northern California, where he was now teaching college, and what we had done over the past thirty years. I decided to send a signal of my attraction to him. I sprawled jokingly across his lap. He enjoyed it, but was careful not to overly respond. He did tell me, "I didn't know that it was possible, but you're more beautiful than you were in high school."

Want to melt a woman's heart, guys? There's your line to use.

Then we talked about spirituality, in which he'd been steeped for more than twenty years, following a yoga meditation tradition that also included a strong Christianity basis. This was not the normal topic for me at a bar, but we formed an immediate bond, a strong bond of some odd nature.

We exchanged e-mails. "I'll definitely keep in touch; will you?" he asked.

"I'd love to."

I thought little of it. I was dealing with the unknown with regard to what was causing my physical weakness. Even though I was my normal spirited and happy self, there was an underlying deep concern. He sensed it for what it was: Something was amiss with my body, and I was feeling and fearing my own mortality.

One other thing: Bob not only loved music in all its forms, but he'd written a book with one of the great ballad singers of our generation, Rock & Roll Hall of Famer Marty Balin of Jefferson Airplane and Jefferson Starship. He had also edited the American Idol magazine during the show's greatest seasons, when Carrie Underwood won it all.

Music and men . . . . are you beginning to see a pattern?

My abdomen was still causing me further alarm. I had a battery of tests, and in June, I underwent a full hysterectomy to remove a cancerous uterine tumor the size of a grapefruit. Just before that, Bob drove 550 miles to see me at a gig by the same band, this time in Carlsbad. He also handed me one of his poetry books, *Shades of Green.* I couldn't believe it; who would drive for eleven hours to see someone with whom he'd just reacquainted? Yes, he got a lot more of my attention.

During our e-mails, I related to him my fears and concerns of the prognoses. I had surely experienced worse, but I hadn't known ahead of time, so there was no fear. I'd also had a husband and family to assist me, but now I had to face it alone.

Bob had taken meticulous care of himself since his late twenties: no smoking, no drinking, no meat, and no drugs. My nerdy little high school friend had become a marathon runner and highly successful high school track and cross-country coach. He knew a lot about diet and nutrition, and sent me a list of books to read on how to strengthen myself through diet. I read one of those books, *Juicing for Life,* and found many ways to build up my blood count and strengthen my immunity. The doctors were amazed at how quickly and wonderfully I healed. While their original instructions were to spend four weeks of bed rest, I was taking short walks around my neighborhood at two weeks with two other old classmates, Joel White and Donny Allen, who drove out to check up on me. You can't keep this girl down! (Sadly, we lost Donny to a car accident in 2015; what a heartbreaking moment.)

My long recovery time off from work came in handy for another reason: My mother's health was failing fast. I visited with her daily during the last two weeks of her life. We laughed, we cried, and we traveled down memory lane of our life and hers when she was a girl. Have you ever seen someone close to you die? It really is a beautiful thing if you can somehow get past the anguish. I hadn't been able to make it to my dad's passing in time, but when I walked into the hospital room in which he lay, his mouth was gaping open. I walked past my mom and my brothers and said, "Oh Daddy, those Angels take your breath away, don't they?"

Now it was my mom's turn. She was home, and her process was slower. One day, she would sort of drift away and rest peacefully, then be back and herself again. On her last day, she was in and out of consciousness, her eyes rolling back in her head, her breath shallow. Suddenly, she opened her eyes wide and stared past us at something, a smile on her face, a sparkle in her eyes. "Mom, it's so beautiful over there, isn't it?" I asked softly.

She looked at me, softly smiled, and reverently nodded her head.

Shortly after that, at the end of July, Mom passed.

In August, Bob returned for a visit to Carlsbad, and we walked on the beach hand-in-hand. The next day, I took him to Balboa Park in San Diego for a more formal date to celebrate his coming birthday. I had gotten us tickets to the art gallery to view the "Musicians in Art" exhibit. Music . . . of course. We enjoyed a picnic on a grassy knoll in Balboa Park, my favorite place, during which we rolled down the hill like a couple of kindergartners. There's a story behind that. We shared a really sweet, innocent history: We were nap pad buddies in kindergarten, and I was his protector (since he was then much shorter than me).

Now, I was beginning to feel the roles reversing. I had always admired his mind, and as everyone around me knows, I love smart men; they will always turn my head first. He was a smart puppy from day one. When I would push all the kindergarten kids on the merry-go-round, Bob would always go right to the middle, so he wouldn't be thrown off when I spun it too fast, my favorite past time as a bratty five-year-old tomboy.

However, something weighed on my mind. In two days, the day before Bob's birthday, my mother's funeral would take place. My siblings chose me to eulogize her. What would I say? I was totally lost. As a book author and editor, it didn't take long for him to figure it out. He calmly said, "Tell me about some highlights of your life with your mom."

I rambled on while he listened and took notes. Not only did he listen to my words, but he also watched my expressions and tuned into my tone of voice. In other words, he listened like a writer. When I finished, he said, "Give me a couple of minutes."

Within five minutes, he handed me an outline for the eulogy. I couldn't believe it: He'd somehow turned my Balboa Park ramble into an organized ebb and flow of everything that mattered to me about my mother and our relationship. He broke it out so I would be telling stories, not just reciting rote memories. Think I didn't notice the correlation between old friend, new lover, writer, and editor? *Thank you God . . . you sent him to guide me through and edit the book I promised to write!*

One other thing: He made me write out the final eulogy. He wouldn't take that final step. I probably wouldn't have let him, but the fact he was insistent really impressed me. Looking back now, I see what was on his mind—*I'll help you with your book, baby doll, but you have to write it.* Ahh . . . Providence.

Ten minutes later, we stood at the long, reflecting pool at Balboa Park, watching lily pads and koi fish floating blissfully. That's when I told him about my accident, and my time in Heaven. At first, he was stunned, and then he smiled warmly. Through his prayer and meditation practices, and Love of Christ, he understood what I said more than just about anyone I'd told.

My eulogy combined the two parts people say they love most about my personality—depth of heart, and humor. I smiled as I delivered it. I referenced a few points of Heaven, mostly that I knew my mom would be with an Angel. It's so odd when you're trying to say something wonderful about a place, where you know any words you use to describe it will pale to any comparison you might describe. But this eulogy was more about the strength of my mother, and all the adventures to which she treated us kids by constantly having us on the go. These were traits I inherited as I developed into a mother of my sons. When I spoke at Dad's funeral, I had talked about his belief in God and his spiritual awareness. I had gladly shared with the people present that he would be going to Heaven, meeting with God, the Divine, and would be engulfed in God's Love forever.

Now both of my parents were gone. I felt like an orphan. I thought it strange that we don't really understand the strength and nurturing we receive from our parents until they are gone. It also didn't escape me that both my parents now resided in the glorious place I'd visited before either of them . . . and to which I wanted to return so badly.

After Mom's funeral and a great week with Bob, I'll never forget him reaching in toward me as he told me that he thought we had something. "That's great," I said, "but you still go back and forth between Kentucky and Northern California."

"I'm a writer; I can live anywhere. I've been planning to move back here anyway. I'll be back."

I'll believe that when I see it, I thought to myself.

Three weeks later, on Labor Day, he knocked on my door. After an incredible twenty-minute kiss on the doorstep, one any man or woman longs for, I let my new man in.

A few months later, we spent a fabulous Christmas in San Francisco, where we walked through Golden Gate Park in a torrential downpour, toured the spectacular architecture gem of the Conservatory of Flowers, and shared a badly needed café latte at a warm, dry coffee house. After changing into dry clothes, we enjoyed a completely unique Christmas meal at an Indian restaurant in Haight-Ashbury, watching Bollywood movies in the back room of the restaurant all to our selves. How about that for a multi-cultural Christmas? We felt as silly, carefree and crazy as the school playmates we used to be.

With Bob and his healthy lifestyle now in my life, I focused anew on stretching and exercise, learning about deep breathing, very little drinking, and switching to a primarily vegetarian diet. I began to feel alive. I had been a vegetarian in my twenties, but quickly switched in the early 1980s when I realized I was married to a meat-and-potatoes guy. I loved this new clean way my body and mind were feeling again.

Bob moved in that December; along with him came hundreds of books. Many of his books dealt with spirituality and religion. At least one book on every major religion sat on his shelves. I remember thinking, *By gosh, God, you've done it again, this is one more of your providential meetings, a love to fill my heart and a writing teacher to help motivate me to get past my fear of writing.* The fear stemmed from my dyslexia. I flashed back to high school, when the teacher questioned me about my dyslexia—in front of the class. I was crushed; I'd carefully kept it from my classmates for all twelve years of school until she threw it out there. I couldn't believe what happened next: Bob, my classmate at the time, got up, stood nose-to-nose with the teacher, and chastised her for her public criticism. He also defended my raw story writing ability. We were seventeen. Hum . . . our life's experiences are strung together preparing us for the next step, aren't they?

I had never really been introduced to other spiritual teachings beyond non-denominational churches and writings. One of his books I picked up was *Autobiography of a Yogi*, by Paramahansa Yogananda, and the other was *The Holy Science*, by Swami Sri Yukteswar. This small book became my favorite. It described astral heaven and gave actual scientific explanations of energy that were so . . . very much the experience I had. But yoga as a spiritual practice? I wasn't so sure about that. In high school, I practiced hatha yoga for its physical benefits. At the time, I didn't know that yoga had any spiritual background. Meditation is not something I did knowingly; however, I have practiced my own version throughout most of my life. I simply referred to it as my reflection time; all I knew was that it gave me peace, calm, and clarity. I have used it in my work and business dealings often.

In Spring 2011, Bob asked if I'd like to get away to the yoga retreat and attached college where he had begun teaching the previous year. We traveled to his cozy little professor's hideaway in Northern California. It felt like *Gilligan's Island,* with rich pine and oak forests instead of water. The intentional community behind it all, Ananda, was much more than I expected. The retreat-turned-college campus sits in the Sierra Nevada foothills in gold rush country, filled with hundreds of ponderosa and sugar pine trees, century-old Manzanita bushes standing six feet high, and the lush green valley floors. The Yuba River rushes through its basin, and the sound echoes through the air. This place is off the grid and runs on generators and well water, and serenity. The people are diverse, kind, gentile, and always polite. They come from many different religions and life paths. They view each other by who they are, inside and out, not what they own or drive. I really enjoyed that perspective, quite different from the Southern California I came from.

However, I was not so excited to hear they followed yogis, rather than God or Jesus; that is, until I visited the temple and looked at the altar. Five portraits pitched toward the middle like a mountain. Four were of yogis entrusted to this path for the past 150 years, but the portrait on top was that of Jesus Christ. *Okay . . . so . . . Jesus is the center focus. This I can grasp.*

I opened my mind to a greater possibility, kind of like a Catholic opening their mind to the thoughts and beliefs of an Episcopalian, Mormon, Baptist, what have you, and vice versa. On my second trip up, Bob was teaching full time and dealing with finals week. The college was in a bustle of readiness for the Christmas break; many parents would be coming to visit or retreat on the property. During my stay, I let one of the ladies know I had decorated for Christmas professionally. I learned quickly that if you don't want to practice Karma Yoga, don't let your volunteer side show. Karma Yoga is sharing your love for God and the God in others through service. Well, it was Christmas, so what better way to share God's Love than to decorate for one of His most important days? This was another providential moment, using my life's experiences so I would feel part of everything, and be of service in this way to glorify Him.

The boxes came down from the rafters and I went to work, dressing the tree, pinning sashes of saris from India on the windows, and decorating the tabletops for the fine dinner to include the many parents and the community. With some sadness, I had to leave to return home to work. I truly enjoyed the shared community caring, and I wanted to take the calmness with me. Again I had a new charged interest in learning more; rather, I felt a need to learn more. And this was, after all, a college . . .

My first experience with Eastern religion took place many years before Ananda, on a beautiful, sparkling day in 1974. My best friend, Marcelle, and I were hitch hiking down the California coast to her home in Cardiff. This was an almost daily trek for us, each day after school. It was June, the last month of school, and we were so elated because our freshman year of high school was almost over. We wanted to grab all the summer fun, music, and teenage girl mystical stuff we possibly could.

Twenty minutes after hitching a ride, we jumped out of the decrepit VW Bug. Our rather funky, older, surfing-bum driver dropped us off in front of the Self-Realization Fellowship Temple, because his destination was the surf spot next door, appropriately named "Swamis." The Self-Realization Center was a magnificent white eastern-styled building, its dormitories reflecting the Spanish architecture that abounded in Southern California during its construction in the mid-1930s. Beautiful, cobalt-blue tiles and a gleaming gold dome at the entrance added to its remarkable charm and sense of tranquility. Neither of us knew anything about the center or what its teachings were. All we knew was the tale of a swami who had come from India in 1920 to bring another variation of God's teachings. The place had the most stunning public gardens, a serpentine layout of native and exotic trees, shrubs, and smaller interior gardens dotted with eastern and Asian influences. There were Koi ponds filled with orange, black, white, big, and tiny fish. Several wonderful Japanese sand raking gardens featured small sculptures of temples and houses, each laced with perfectly placed little bonsai trees.

We had passed by this intriguing place too many times to count, but had only actually entered the garden a few times. While the gardens were open to the public, the monastery's large, protective, vine-covered walls made us feel like we shouldn't go in. This time we could hear chanting and singing, and we had peeked over the stucco walls to get a glimpse of who was doing the chanting. It turned out to be a cluster of orange-robed monks of varying ages and sizes. Something about these monks was welcoming, yet it seemed like we were sneaking, like we were intruders who, if we got caught, would be busted. Nevertheless, being girls with eyes wide open, we saw three young teenaged and good-looking monks, so naturally we wanted to know more.

We strolled slowly toward our targets, nonchalantly looking at the trees and flowers, weaving our way through the garden, and casually stopping to take a closer look at a flower or a koi pond. All along, we had a single intention: to reach the young monks in those bright orange robes by walking across the Japanese raking garden.

We smiled and paused nearby, waiting for some kind of a greeting. It was apparent that these boy monks were shy, or so we thought. We figured we would need to prompt some interest out of them, so we giggled, flashed bright smiles, walked closer with our scantily clad, tanned, California surfer-girl bodies, and asked for their names, with our eyes shining. They almost froze in place. A brown-skinned guy with an unusual accent greeted us with a wide smile and dewy brown eyes. "Good Day, ladies." The other two nodded, but we could see their intrigue, even through the quiet and restrained manner they possessed.

Naturally, we noticed their looks first. One was a perfectly flawless tall blond with an all-American, athletic look, actually from a Scandinavian country. He caught our attention in the first place. The second guy was gorgeous, an Asian with the sweetest smile. The third monk, our greeter with the dark skin and thick accent, came from India. All of the guys looked like they were in their late teens or early twenties. We walked and talked about what they were doing, why they were drawn to be monks and live at this ashram, and how it worked to be part of a spiritual walk, or quest. They each explained how their lives had been before joining the ashram; it was so close to what we were going through ourselves.

We were becoming more open, and even a little fresh, when one of them suggested he show us how to meditate. We sat in the sunlit garden, trying not to stir, but it was futile. The energy between very warm-blooded young girls and strange young guys was too strong. Our efforts came to an end when their mentor, leader, or headmaster, I'm not sure what he was called, walked up. He didn't want them speaking with us.

Wow . . . so much peace and calm from teenage boys. This was new. Each was so different from the other, in their looks, voices and accents, but their demeanor was very similar. It was the demeanor that drew in Marcelle and me; they had an inner flow that suggested more knowledge and wisdom than they could have possibly possessed at such a young age. Or could they?

I was introduced to meditation and eastern spirituality at Ananda. And guess what? The same yogis' faces were there; it was the same path Marcelle and I had stumbled onto. Then, I was fifteen. Now, I was fifty. Again, it was a guy who drew me in. However, I had a greater view of my inner spirituality, many years of biblical studies, a taste of Heaven, and had read a transformative bestselling book, *Embraced by the Light* by Betty J. Eadie. I had also started looking into mediation and its teachings. I had read only a few books on meditation, and I knew very little about the actual practice. Bob taught me a few techniques, but I was still such a rookie; I didn't know what I was doing. I only knew that the peace from those monks many years back was the same peace I saw in Bob after he meditated. I wanted it to be a part of my life.

During our stay over the Christmas holiday, one morning was clear, crisp, and not too cold. We headed for a little underground nook called Babaji Cave (named for one of India's most revered yoga masters) to meditate. The cave is small, dark, and damp with enough room for maybe five people. Bob played the harmonium, an Indian instrument similar to a small organ. He guided me through a few breathing exercises, and then we went deep into meditation.

While I was gone from all thought, a picture, bright and vivid in color and form, lit up my forehead. In yogic teachings, the spiritual eye is located at the point between the eyebrows; this is also called the Christ Center. Jesus was no stranger to yogic teachings, according to many "lost" books of the Bible, even alluded to directly in Matthew 6:22: "If thine eye be single, thy body shall be full of light." Within my spiritual eye shone a clear picture of an elegantly decorated half-elephant, half-man. I tried to get him to go away; I didn't know what was going on. I felt very peaceful about the whole thing, but it was very foreign to me.

Later, I learned more about this elephant-man, Ganesh, a revered Hindu God, the Lord of Success and Destroyer of Obstacles. The son of the god and goddess Shiva and Parvati, he was critically injured and his life saved, but he was given a new head. The only one available was that of an elephant. Ganesh's head symbolizes the *Atman* or the soul, the supreme reality of human existence, and his human body represents *Maya*, or our earthly existence. The elephant head connotes wisdom and its trunk represents Om, the sound symbol of cosmic reality—one I heard so richly in Heaven.

After the mediation, I explained my vision of this strange elephant man to Bob. He marveled at my instant perception and "visitation" from such a deity.

When learning to walk, I would joke that I wanted to feel God's gentle tap on my shoulder, rather than the sledgehammer.

I was incredibly stressed about work; it was taking its toll on me. I wanted more; rather, I *needed* more. I still couldn't find a renewed connection to why I had come back to this life. My boys were now grown and they didn't need a mother's attention, and my job certainly wasn't feeding anything except the salesmen's pockets. I yearned for my day-to-day existence to have greater meaning, a higher purpose, to better utilize the lessons of Heaven.

Once again, God provided providence, but this time, it wasn't as easy to recognize as a blessing.

In February 2011, I enjoyed fantastic sales-retention numbers at work, the best any manager had achieved for some time. Still, my boss pressured me (yet again) to lay off one of my three staff members. I couldn't find a worthwhile reason; their numbers were fine. One had just become a new father, and another was paying for two daughters in college. I offered up the guy that was the lowest performer and newest addition as the sacrificial lamb, feeling he didn't really deserve to lose his job, either. However, he was lucky enough to be part of the "good old boy" team with this boss. If I didn't fire one of the other two, he told me, I would lose my job. *Why?* My team's cancelation numbers were at 11% in an industry where 18% to 20% is average, and people don't get fired until they are at or above 30%.

A few weeks after that unpleasant discussion with my boss, I drove to work after depositing a small inheritance check from my mom's estate. I walked inside—and learned I had been replaced. *What?* My cold-hearted boss actually had the gall to carry out his threat. Who replaced me? Someone close to the higher ups—it's not always what you know but who you know. I was now let go from my job, joining millions of others looking for work in a terrible job market. Plus, I was a fifty-two-year-old Caucasian female without a college degree. It would have made a sad country song . . . and I was shedding plenty of tears.

The next year couldn't have been tougher. With my boys in college, I passed through my first year of unemployment in a daze. I don't believe my soul has ever been so damaged as it was by that simple action of being fired, because I felt rejected, and I took it as my not being mentally capable. I had worked so hard, scratched my way back to normal. But now I asked, what is normal? I had the struggle of trying to hang on to my home, the only thing I received after twenty-one years of marriage (along with its five hundred thousand mortgage, which unemployment wouldn't even make a scratch on).

I realized that my best move was to let go of the family home in a short sale. While my sons, brothers and Bob carried everything into the moving van, I looked in the mirror and realized that, after many fantastic years of a fabulous life, I now owned nothing. I wanted to cry, but instead I realized I was *smiling*. I thought of Heaven, and realized another reality about Eternity: All we really get to take with us is our memories and our integrity. I looked into the mirror and thought, *Hey, honey, you don't arrive in Heaven with a moving van; remember, no U-Hauls allowed.*

I never really held much importance to things, even though I certainly possessed enough of them. When I packed everything up, I realized how much I no longer needed or had a desire to own. I believe in perseverance, in getting up each time we fall, and most of all not giving in to despair. I tell myself there is a part of us, our soul, that tells us "we decide" what we're going to create in our life, or rather we "will" it to happen, and it *will* happen every single time . . . without exception, if we believe enough. This pattern of thought can be dangerous if kept that simple, because it takes something else—follow-through.

Ever since I took my first steps on Christmas Eve 1999, I'd heard a mantra I placed first and foremost in my mind and I recited it when life grew tough: *I can, I shall, I will! I can dance in my own spotlight, I shall create my individual life; I will bask in the light of my abilities within.* I needed to reach deep into my soul for strength and pull myself up by my bootstraps yet again.

As I continue to wonder what I will do next in life, I know every opportunity holds a mystery and a potential, and I get to decide how I will address it. I believe we have complete control over how we see our world, and the meanings we give things. How we choose to look at things as they happen is our choice. We can choose to make it ugly—or beautiful. So as it were I chose to consider my ten square-meter storage unit that housed my furniture as my new home. I just wasn't going to live there. I packed up and decided to make the choice that everything was going to be beautiful.

Chapter 19

Back to School . . .

and Birthing a Book

"Knowledge is power," my daddy always told me. With every material aspect of my former life now removed, I put his wisdom to the test.

In 2012, I returned to college, some thirty years after last attending full-time. I moved to Northern California, to Ananda College where I saw many growth opportunities through the classes offered. I was searching for the knowledge that had poured into me while I was with the Trinity, the search that will continue for the rest of my life. The fact I had not been a student for such a long time was daunting. However, a kid in a candy store couldn't hold more excitement than me about this opportunity. I knew how proud my pops would be of my returning to college and working on the first pass at this book.

Books were part of what made my dad's heart beat. He vicariously traveled through many lands, experienced many adventures, and embraced many romances via the white pages bound between two covers. Now it was my turn. Dad beamed down upon me from Heaven, I'm sure smiling with utter joy. I imagined him holding the fountain of knowledge, and pouring it into my brain and soul, just as my Heavenly Father had done. One of the highest qualities he instilled in me was such a thirst for knowledge.

Within a week of arriving in the Sierra Nevada foothills, something else struck me: what a perfect place for my wounded soul to heal!

As they say, life comes in phases (like the seven-year phase). My phase *was* seven years, from the time of my divorce until returning to college. So much had happened, been stripped away, and now it was truly a new beginning. I actually enjoyed the lack of a job. Money and things meant little to my fellow students and faculty.

I decided to live every moment to the fullest, starting by a daily walk in the woods along the "Four-Mile Loop," a track of fire road, deer trail, and hard-packed soil. I searched my thoughts and feelings, trying to find me, the real me, not the one with financial worries. Some of the girls worried I would encounter a bear, but since I hold no fear of death, a lil' old black bear wasn't going to stop me. I looked straight to the ground, maneuvering the narrow, twisting path with its incline, and heard a grunt. I glanced up, and there was a big, eight-point black tail buck deer, the largest I've ever seen, showing off his gorgeous antlers.

This started something truly amazing. Almost every morning after our first encounter, he would wait for me in the meadow behind our little six-hundred-square-foot round house, situated among a grove of ponderosas and black oaks. When I hiked up the hill to class, he often greeted me. One morning, he paused maybe six feet away, stared at me with his black eyes, and licked his muzzle with his black tongue. A pretty forward and enticing way of saying good morning! Then he bounded down the bank with his half-dozen does trailing behind. He was quite the harem's man. I started to refer to him as my boyfriend, and it seemed like, in his way of looking at it, he added me to his group.

The guys from class couldn't believe what they were seeing, that he didn't feel threatened by or charge me. "He likes me," I told them. This was their first encounter with another "little extra" that came back with me from Heaven: my ability to communicate immediately and meaningfully with animals.

Still, I was amazed: Why did this buck befriend me so closely? Charles, the charming keeper of our amazing two-acre tree, plant, and flower garden, told me our campus sat atop a sacred Maidu Indian burial ground. He added that it was a high energy vortex, in part because something else lay a few hundred feet further down: one of the largest untapped gold reserves in the world. When gold prices started spiking in 2010, the hill on which we studied became the subject of an ongoing dogfight between hungry mining companies and local conservationists, led by our next-door neighbor and friend, the Pulitzer Prize-winning poet Gary Snyder. As such, Charles said, the energy of the place might feel odd at first. Odd? This was a little too much. Let's see . . . first I find myself meditating with a visit from Ganesh, half human with a elephant head. Now I'm a best buddy with a wild buck deer. All things, animals, plants, and humans are interconnected, right?

Another thing that resulted from my accident was that I wanted to understand why things were happening to me. I wanted to reach the prize (so to speak) faster. I wanted to quickly learn what I was supposed to do, what I was supposed to attain, and why I wasn't getting there. I looked at the students, faculty, and location . . . *what I'm supposed to attain.* These people were entirely receptive to my experience of Heaven. Not only that, but they wanted to know more. I'd found my place of rehearsal of speaking publicly.

One of my classes was creative writing. When the semester started, our professor told us that, if we had a particular project we wanted to work on—say, a memoir—that we could use the entire course to develop it. He would tailor the course requirements to work within our purposeful writing projects, while also having us sharpen our pencils with a few outside essays. When I heard this, the Angels almost trumpeted in my ears. What a Godsend! I planned on taking advantage of it. I sat at a college full of students from differing spiritual backgrounds, nationalities, and ages on this plot of land on the North San Juan Ridge. This was the true gold mine for me. There wouldn't be a better place, or *time,* to write a manuscript with such single-minded focus. Plus, the community could help guide me. I sat at the crossroads of these paths, as well as my promise to God—to tell my story to the whole world. I started writing.

Our community of students and faculty shared meals together (not exactly the way it is anymore, at campuses *or,* sadly, at many home dinner tables). As we ate, I began to open up and relate more and more of my story with the group. I found that their minds were far more open and their levels of acceptance much greater than many of those back home. Back in Pauma Valley, I was often expected to not mention it at all, or to keep my thoughts and stories in rigid lock-step with what a host group's view of Heaven may be. Any misstep, and I would be abruptly, sometimes rudely, put in my place. Here, I was thrilled that they not only believed my story, but also saw it as a beacon to a place they wanted to attain through their meditation practices.

Likewise, I felt a need to expand my horizons and more deeply understand beliefs outside my non-denominational Christian practices, and see what lay beyond them. I had seen first-hand that God and the loving vibrancy of Heaven was far more than the box that religions try to place it into. I appreciate religion and the need that many people have for their organization, leadership, and focused direction, but what I saw in Heaven was ever so much more. It cannot be named, it cannot be contained.

I loved how everything at the campus related to Heaven and, ultimately, to Jesus, the Heavenly Father and even the feminine aspect of God, the Divine Mother. Not surprisingly, the group was enthralled by my story, and it wasn't just the students but many of the community elders—they asked questions, and usually followed up my answers by digging for more details. They wanted to *know* what consciousness and perception would be like on the other side. These conversations drew me into places that really gave this book its first wings. This gave me the courage to really write my story. Their inquires would prepare me for the more interesting and reflective questions such as:

What is your unique perspective on your NDE?

Well . . . I now believe in them! I laughingly say this, but it's no joke. Prior to my accident, I didn't believe in Angels, and I thought of near-death experiences as hocus-pocus, not a reality. Doctors tried to tell me they were flashes caused by the dying brain, but I know I was literally in Heaven and I did communicate with my Angel and the Divinity of God.

Why do so many people find it hard to believe someone can have a near-death experience, a taste of eternity, or have direct perception of God?

Because we are too busy judging. Judgment causes the unbearable fear of non-acceptance. From our first day on the playground, all we want is to be accepted, part of the group, and invited in. Some people can't accept what they haven't seen, touched or felt themselves. Some need science to prove anything or everything before they will accept it. Often, people are afraid that society will think them odd or mentally off.

What is the one strongest impression that you came away with?

The overwhelming purity of Love that surrounded me. I only wish I could find one fraction of this here on Earth. By far, the strongest impression was Love. Love filled every bit of every cell of creation. Think of the pounding energy of the ocean and how refreshed you feel just walking next to it, your spirit is filled with Love. Think of its waves spilling over you with all that Love.

What about other impressions?

There were a couple. There was my understanding of God's mastery of the finite: The design of every living cell and particle is truly amazing. Think of the perfection that occurs in nature over and over again. Look at the mathematical perfection of a sunflower, a conch shell, a pinecone or pineapple. This is not a coincidence. Consider the perfect spiral or Golden Ratio, otherwise known as PHI, in the shape of an egg, the ear, a galaxy like the Milky Way. God reveals himself in Nature, in everything around us, every plant, and flower of our world. They are part of God's Divine power. Also, there is a intercommunication between humans and plants. It was astounding to see this.

I also have a deeper need for Truth. Truthfulness is the most important aspect of Love, and Love is the essence of our souls.

Another impression was this: When you are in Heaven, your soul is completely unveiled. The Divine sees and knows everything about us, having created and designed our full lives in an exquisite master plan, which we call destiny. I felt all God wanted from me was to be purely me, myself only, with no hidden agendas or thoughts. He could read them anyway.

Finally, I wish I could see a rainbow on earth displayed with the same Technicolor spectrum of living, singing, vibrating colors that I saw in Heaven. Our rainbow colors here are really just muddy colors in comparison.

And finally, my favorite question: *What would you like people to take away from your experience?*

The Golden Rule: *Do unto others as you would have them do unto you.* Giving, sharing, and expressing love are the most important gifts we have to offer! Love is the only eternal possession we have. When we die, the only thing we take with us is the love we shared, the memories we make, and our integrity. Everything else stays here.

Six weeks into the semester, I joined a few others for a month-long pilgrimage to India, the cradle of yoga, Sanskrit, and many religions. Some claim it to be a place where Jesus visited during his "lost years" when the Bible has no record of his whereabouts.

Namaste—it begins. I visited various places of Christian, Buddhist, Sikh, and Hindu worship, including Mother Theresa's "Mission of Charity" Orphanage and Gandhi's Museum and Memorial, and the Sikh's amazing Golden Temple in Amistar, Varanasi—the Hindu City of Shiva—to see the fantastic Arati on the shores of Ma Ganga. We proceeded to Sarnath, where Buddha gave his first lecture, and then the Bodhi tree and its temples at Bodh Gaya, where Gautama Buddha became enlightened twenty-five centuries ago. Of course, we visited the Taj Mahal in Agra, built in 1531.

To finalize our travels, we attended the Dalai Lama's annual pilgrimage speaking engagement at Dharamsala, where I mingled with the masses. There certainly was no shortage of masses, anywhere in this packed country of over one billion people.

I was feeling whole again. I read everything I could get my hands on, anything I felt would relate to my story during those long, twelve- to eighteen-hour train rides from one side of the country to the other.

When I got back to the Sierras, I dug in and wrote. This was a perfect start to *The Fragrance of Angels*.

No matter the growing number of related books on the shelves, the question remains hotly debated: Is there life after death, or is life over when we die? Do we proceed to a place of indescribable beauty, as described in religious texts? Or do we just cease to exist?

There is more beyond the quality of life we are living right now. It has been suggested that people who have had NDEs encounter a new type of consciousness, increased spirituality, but separate from church-going religiousness. They desire to be more tolerant of people's idiosyncrasies, and try to appreciate how all living things relate and connect. I have seen this in personal friends who have had their own NDEs; we share an awe of what we saw, and not one of us will deny it happened—nor what we saw, for that matter.

Certainly, I would love for my NDE to hold a purpose and value beyond my own personal growth. I believe most of our small portion of the population that has seen the magnificent light of Heaven and returned strive to do just that, to share it somehow—some way. Many believe that our experiences may be revelations into a divine dimension. Hum . . . a Divine Dimension, I agree!

When I look back at my NDE, I try to share my experience and suggest possible answers that may enhance someone's view of death, life after death, the soul, or our higher purpose in life. This is a question that only each individual person can answer for himself or herself. We are all our own unique selves. My answer may not be the next person's, but it doesn't make one of us right and the other wrong. What about questions like, "Why have I chosen the life I live?" "Do we have the Free Will to determine our life paths?" "Did we super-consciously make these decisions before entering this life?" Meaning did I actually choose to be

Martha Halda, and consciously decide to go through this before I was even born?

People who have had NDEs often spend the rest of their lives trying to make sense of experiences for which science and religion have poorly prepared them. We have the task of deciding what our meaning, understanding, or mission is in relation to what we were shown. Most people aren't living the life that hits the mark of what they ultimately want. So often, people don't think of our greater purpose or value until we're near the end of our lives; then we want another chance. After my NDE, I realized I will have to live within my truth, always; it can be unbearable to change to suit society.

It's an agonizing process, especially when I need to drop some of my guilty pleasures or past ways to arrive at a new, greater understanding of life. I actually like my glass of wine or bowl of ice cream, even when I know firsthand that my body, mind, and soul run better and are more clear when I don't indulge in them. An even greater challenge is when I react to someone in a negative way. Unbearable. I fear the review that will come with it.

My drive is to live a healthy, spiritually directed life, yet I am not church-like. It begins by switching from an outer to inner focus, which I did at Ananda. I enjoyed the 6 a.m. group meditations, which I viewed as my Morning Prayer group, only more concentrated and silent. I loved how my new friends viewed religion; they went right to the origins to find the points in common between *all* religions. I am absolutely a Christian; Jesus Christ is the Divine holy teacher, my guru I choose to follow in this life. However, I completely honor other religions and believe that the God Energy I experienced in Heaven would not condemn anyone for following their own religion, with the depth of their heart and the example of their actions. If it's a path of Divine Love, it works for me. If it's not, then it's probably different than it was originally taught in the first place—and I veer away from it.

Sometimes, I'm asked, "How can you say you're a Christian, if you don't think people must only follow Jesus?" That's a very good question, but I don't know what other people will be judged for in their review; I can only speak to my own. My reply: "Each person may have a moment in their life review when their personal good life and good deeds are noted, and perhaps they are offered that final moment of acceptance of Jesus. I have no way of knowing what God holds for other people."

Those thoughts billowed within me every day as I planned my chapters, caught sunset at nearby Bald Mountain, tilled the gardens soil, and walked the Four-Mile Loop.

The other part of my college experience was karma yoga—physical service to God, performed with complete gratitude. How hard is it to plant vegetables, till gardens and feed chickens daily in a gorgeous mountain foothill setting? It was awesome, and I always served with a huge smile on my face and in my heart. This part God made really easy for me.

Meanwhile, Bob, a marathon runner, motivated me to run along the hillsides and beautiful trails. During the spring, I ran a pair of 5Ks, actually *ran* them, my first since . . . well, college! In 2003, I had power walked but not run the Dublin Marathon, and averaged a fifteen-minute mile. Now, in 2012, I felt so healthy and recovered from the accident that we did the 5K Tulip Race in a nearby town. I won the open walk-run, averaging faster than ten minutes per mile—a total shocker! We made it a couple's daily double, as Bob won the fifty to fifty-nine men's division. To top this off, I have since run/walked two different half marathons, one in Missoula, Montana, and the other in my hometown of Carlsbad. These races reconfirmed that the strongest muscle in the human body consists of the six inches between our ears. Our brain. Belief and willpower can carry us a long way.

Back in class, one of our writing projects was to write a poem in a style the professor termed, "zoom in, zoom out." I sat on a bluff and wrote what I saw, felt, heard, and smelled. The point was to write what I observed from a hundred feet away, then fifty feet, then ten feet, and so on. A literary night presentation was coming up, in which students read their works or showcased their art to the hundred or so people who attended. I had no art, not anything I was going to willingly share in public. I had painted my version of Vincent Van Gogh's *The Starry Night*, but it wasn't finished yet. Therefore, I decided I would need to share my zoom-in, zoom-out poem/stream of consciousness writing about Bald Mountain.

It's a beautiful, glisteningly sunlit day in April, out here on Bald Mountain.

Zooming into my senses, and see what I can feel:
I'm sitting, perched, embedding myself on a grand old bolder of the California gold rush. It's encrusted with a lime-colored crystalline-type moss, whose name I can't recall. This bold, chilled gray stone offers both comfort and a feeling of warmth to my legs and tush.

Zooming out about five feet:
Below me, waves of oxen-colored twists of Manzanita topped with puffs of sage-colored leaves send a deep, rusty oil smell to my face. The smell is rather fragrant, almost sweet, and yet a hint of bitterness, like an old dark chocolate. The leaves rustle softly in the breeze.

Zooming out yet again—this time a hundred feet:
I see the silvery blush of the current's flow on the Yuba River. I realize the whispers of the wind are actually the rushing sounds of this far-off, love-filled river. She has a personality of her own. The river, this sweet lady is sounding her welcome of hello to me. I relax, stop thinking, stop moving, and just listen. I hear the gods sending me their hello, enveloping me in their cradling caresses of wind, warmth, and Nature so pure!

Zooming farther:
The bees buzzing, the chirping songs of birds, the breeze blowing softly through the pines. The wind whirls across the valley, blowing atop the large, protective trees I've grown to know and love. Sending rushing sounds that remind me of the crashing waves of home.

Zooming this time gone deep into my heart and soul:
Waves, ahhh yes . . . how I miss the coastline. The ocean
with its sparkling turquoise sea, laced with white tips
gracing her waves. The smell of the salt air as it fills my
memory. Memories of years spent on her silvery sands.
The sand, wet, damp, chilled, squishing water out from un-
der my feet as I run, ringing out its salty moisture hidden
deep within. I miss the hazy softness that fills the evening
while I sit on the bluffs to watch the setting sun, hoping
to catch the green flash—the flash as the sun's reflection
shines through the ocean's horizon line.

Zooming back . . . up the ridge:
The sunsets here are stunning, full of glorious yellows,
golds, and deep-red wisps of clouds. But the sunsets over
the ocean's horizon are home, a lifetime of memories!
They fill my soul with life, warming me anew with every
sunset I embrace.

After reading this, touched to the core by what poured through my hands and the words I spoke, I choked up in front of everyone. There it was: the way my time in Heaven changed the way I viewed life, written with the comfort I'd gained by being with people who thoroughly embraced me as a soul in a loving and supportive way. This was how I viewed life—zoom in, and zoom out, first at a distance, even unto the heavens, then back to the world in front of my face.

It was time to spread my wings and return home to Southern California to see what new adventures awaited me there.

Beach Reunion

The beautiful August day brought out Southern California at its finest. My sister Katie and I enjoyed the ocean's crystalline teal blue softness, its temperature not much cooler than bath water. We sat on the beach, bodysurfed, and frolicked in the shallow tides with our friend Brenda's grandkids. "You're like a mermaid!" the little girls teased. True enough: I love the freedom of floating in the salty blue water, embracing the beauty of this universe we are all lucky enough to share. I also feel whole, without glitches or handicaps, possessing the perfect, strong body I had in my twenties—well, okay, maybe my forties. I think to myself, maybe these sweet little girls can sense it, as they call me their mermaid. I laugh to myself (or, at myself) and think sometimes my mind is just too simplistic in how I see things full of peace, love, and harmony.

My home environment has always been near the ocean, so this day on the beach was a return to that childlike space of comfort. The waves were big enough to be fun, but not so large to be too much of a workout. Since it was mid-week, the summer crowds were manageable as well.

Katie and I decided we didn't get enough of a workout body-surfing. We took off down the beach for a nice walk, another of my lifelong habits. We strolled and talked, churned over ideas, and shared loves and losses in the way sisters can do. My sister and I reminisced about our childhood on these beaches, how lucky we were to grow up here with our dad serving as a teacher and dean at Army Navy Academy, which borders this beach. Now we celebrated the idea of growing old here, enveloped in the feeling of belonging, of history, of family, of life's learning and lessons.

As we neared the "The Point," a sand spot that, along with Buena Vista Lagoon, divides Carlsbad and Oceanside, I saw a happy couple. They looked familiar, but . . . *No, this isn't their town.* Nor was it a beach they would normally choose. As we moved closer and their faces become clearer, there was no doubt:

It was Rob Gilster, the man who had first stopped and tended to me after my accident.

A big grin engulfed his face, followed by his hearty booming voice: "Hey, it's Marty Lou!"

I started to laugh. "I can't believe it!" Katie was a little confused; what was it that I didn't believe? her eyes suggested. She had never heard anyone ever call me Marty Lou (nor will she; that nickname is for Rob alone). She probably felt it more likely that, if someone called me "Marty Lou," their lives would be in danger!

I ran up and gave Rob and his wife, Robin, a big hug. I was happy to see them. I hadn't seen either for about seven years, since 2005, when our boys graduated from Valley Center High School together. True to his large personality (one that to me sparkles with energy), and very strong sense of community, Rob was not about to allow a mere seven years of time alter our friendship in any way. "I read another book!" he barked out, laughing and smiling.

The comment hovers in the air as if we had talked to each other yesterday. "Wow, another book, great!" I teased. "That makes what, two or three for you?"

He smiled. "Marty Lou, it's called *90 Minutes in Heaven.* Certain parts gave me goose bumps, and I wondered, how much of it is like your story? You know, I think of you all the time and wonder how you are."

That's when my sister figured out who this guy was.

Rob found me lying flattened on a dirt road, smeared in blood and dirt, gasping for breath and life. He watched over me and prayed for me while waiting for the paramedics to arrive. I knew he didn't recognize me on the scene, but I will forever remember his deeply sincere prayers for that woman on the road—the prayers I could feel.

"So Marty Lou, what have you been doing?" Rob asked.

"Well, actually, I'm two days behind my schedule writing my book."

"On?"

"On my taste of eternity."

Robin turned and smiled, the warmth in her eyes making it clear she was deeply impressed. "When are you planning to finish it?"

"I can't tell you, but I'm working hard on it."

We talked for a few more minutes, and then I excused myself. "I need to get busy, but I really believe seeing you guys on the beach is a message from God that I'd better take this writing more seriously," I said.

Seeing Rob and Robin kicked up another Valley Center memory from December 2000, probably the first time since the accident I started to believe I would become a complete, fit woman and person again. On a chilly afternoon, I received the best, absolutely most wonderful compliment of my life while walking the school track at Valley Center Junior High, where Nate had basketball practice. This was during my first year of recovery after the accident; I was diligently trying to click off a mile in that hour of practice. I was mentally beating up myself the entire way about how long it took to cover such a short distance; hadn't I run track in college and clocked seventy-mile training weeks? My healthy athlete's ego was thoroughly bruised by my snail's pace. Never mind the accident. What was that, an excuse for going slower? My body screamed, *hell yes, girl!* I soldiered on like any good athlete.

This day I noticed a kind, older Indian man while walking the track. I'd seen him in Valley Center for years, but we had never met before. We exchanged greetings and small talk about the town, the beauty of Palomar Mountain, and the always-welcomed late-afternoon breeze. After our chat, I returned to my pace and he kept his own. He looked about seventy-five and walked with a cane, but he was upright and pouring himself into his workout. He carried himself with such dignity that he reminded me of Geronimo, the great Bedonkohe Apache warrior.

After he finished his last lap, the man said, "You must be an athlete; you walk like one."

My eyes filled with tears that speed tracked from my heart and soul. He had no idea how wonderful those words sounded. The trickle-down effect once again playing out in life, sometimes we have no idea how a simple sentence we say can bring so much more and mean so much more to the person receiving that comment. It was coming up on one year since I came home to heal, since the doctors had put the rest of Humpty Dumpty back together. When I saw the Indian man, I'd been walking unassisted for about seven months, not far, but certainly not with crutches or leg braces—which, the doctors had warned me, might be the case. Or, worse, that I would be confined to a wheelchair.

No, this man told me the exact opposite: *You must be an athlete.*

I could now sit there on the beach and, in large part, celebrate my complete recovery with Rob and Robin because of that man. He called me an athlete. He lit a fire beneath me. He saw me for who I was in my deeper, essential self, not what the accident had temporarily rendered. Isn't that how we all want to be seen?

An affirmation I'd heard years before and made part of me, of who I am, once again came alive inside me following my walk. I have kept this very close every day since. It speaks to Heaven, earth, how to live in one place while trying to get to the other . . . and how life changes if circumstances (such as bad car accidents) reverse the normal order of things:

I can, I shall, I will! I can dance in my own spotlight, I shall create my individual life, and I will bask in the light of my abilities within. The Kingdom of Heaven is within me.

For a few exalted minutes, it was also around me. And thankfully I was part of it, my taste of eternity.

About the Author

My life can be summed up in four words: faith, family, adventure, and perseverance. My life was built around family, until life crashed to a halt on October 8, 1999. I suffered the car crash that provides the basis for *The Fragrance of Angels.* This taste of eternity is the story of my near-death experience during this near-fatal car accident, and my quest to regain a normal life. Being a former college track and volleyball athlete provided me the drive and skills to regain my strength and survive. Writing this book provides me the outlet to fulfill a promise; to my late father, Ray F. Brookhart, and more importantly to God that I would tell my story and of His Love.

Today, I live Oceanside, California. I encourage people to enjoy the marvels of this world, and to create precious memories with the people who mean the most in their life, because I know that all we get to take with us is our integrity and our memories.

CPSIA information can be obtained
at www.ICGtesting.com
Printed in the USA
FSOW03n2257300816
24364FS